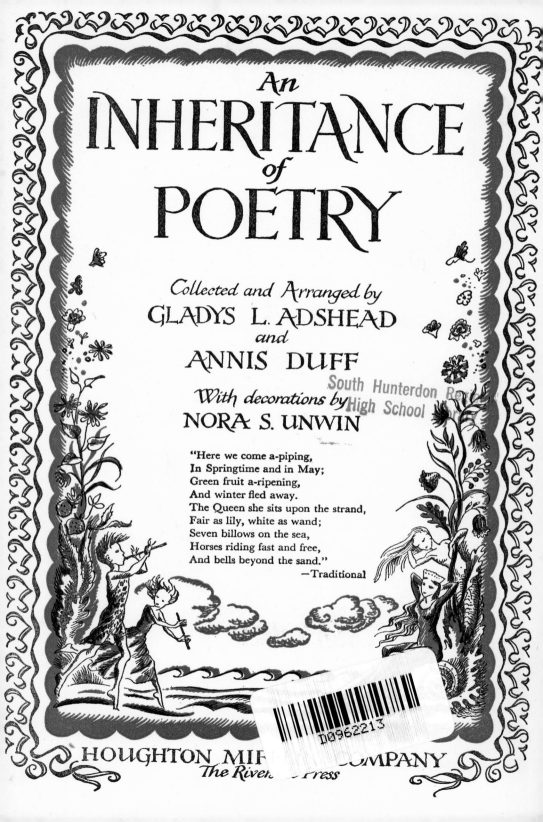

An
INHERITANCE
of
POETRY

Collected and Arranged by
GLADYS L. ADSHEAD
and
ANNIS DUFF

With decorations by
NORA S. UNWIN

"Here we come a-piping,
In Springtime and in May;
Green fruit a-ripening,
And winter fled away.
The Queen she sits upon the strand,
Fair as lily, white as wand;
Seven billows on the sea,
Horses riding fast and free,
And bells beyond the sand."
—Traditional

HOUGHTON MIFFLIN COMPANY
The Riverside Press

COPYRIGHT, 1948, BY
ANNIS DUFF AND GLADYS L. ADSHEAD

ALL RIGHTS RESERVED INCLUDING THE RIGHT
TO REPRODUCE THIS BOOK OR PARTS THEREOF
IN ANY FORM

The Riverside Press
CAMBRIDGE · MASSACHUSETTS
PRINTED IN THE U.S.A.

To **Walter de la Mare**

A poem . . . is a blossoming in words of a language at a certain time in its history, and words stand for things, objects, actions, as well as ideas. It was the work also of one man living in a certain place and period and setting and state of being and often in a bygone century. Is it waste of pains, then, even when one is young, to attempt not only to realize this but to illustrate it in some degree, and so to cross again and again over the slender bridge between poetry and actuality, between the world of the imagination and the world without? There will not be less to be seen on either side by becoming familiar with both of them.

— Walter de la Mare
in *COME HITHER*

I know well that only the rarest kind of best in anything can be good enough for the young.

— Walter de la Mare in *BELLS AND GRASS: Preface*

We have been careful that they that will read may
have delight, and that they that are desirous to
commit to memory might have ease, and that all
into whose hands it comes might have profit.

II Maccabees 2:25

If thou hast gathered nothing in thy youth,
how canst thou find anything in thine age?

Ecclesiasticus 25:3

THE CREATION

And God stepped out on space,
And he looked around and said:
I'm lonely —
I'll make me a world.

And far as the eye of God could see
Darkness covered everything,
Blacker than a hundred midnights
Down in a cypress swamp.

Then God smiled,
And the light broke,
And the darkness rolled up on one side,
And the light stood shining on the other,
And God said: That's good!

Then God reached out and took the light in his hands,
And God rolled the light around in his hands
Until he made the sun;
And he set that sun a-blazing in the heavens.
And the light that was left from making the sun
God gathered it up in a shining ball
And flung it against the darkness,
Spangling the night with the moon and stars.
Then down between the darkness and the light
He hurled the world;
And God said: That's good!

Then God himself stepped down —
And the sun was on his right hand,
And the moon was on his left;
The stars were clustered about his head,

And the earth was under his feet.
And God walked, and where he trod
His footsteps hollowed the valleys out
And bulged the mountains up.

Then he stopped and looked and saw
That the earth was hot and barren.
So God stepped over to the edge of the world
And he spat out the seven seas —
He batted his eyes, and the lightnings flashed —
He clapped his hands, and the thunders rolled —
And the waters above the earth came down,
The cooling waters came down.

Then the green grass sprouted,
And the little red flowers blossomed,
The pine tree pointed his finger to the sky,
And the oak spread out his arms,
The lakes cuddled down in the hollows of the ground,
And the rivers ran down to the sea;
And God smiled again,
And the rainbow appeared,
And curled itself around his shoulder.

Then God raised his arm and he waved his hand
Over the sea and over the land,
And he said: Bring forth! Bring forth!
And quicker than God could drop his hand,
Fishes and fowls
And beasts and birds
Swam the rivers and the seas,
Roamed the forests and the woods,
And split the air with their wings.
And God said: That's good!

Then God walked around,
And God looked around
On all that he had made.
He looked at his sun,
And he looked at his moon,
And he looked at his little stars;
He looked on his world
With all its living things,
And God said: I'm lonely still.

Then God sat down —
On the side of a hill where he could think;
By a deep, wide river he sat down;
With his head in his hands,
God thought and thought,
Till he thought: I'll make me a man!

Up from the bed of the river
God scooped the clay;
And by the bank of the river
He kneeled him down;
And there the great God Almighty
Who lit the sun and fixed it in the sky,
Who flung the stars to the most far corner of the night,
Who rounded the earth in the middle of his hand;
This Great God,
Like a mammy bending over her baby,
Kneeled down in the dust
Toiling over a lump of clay
Till he shaped it in his own image;

Then into it he blew the breath of life,
And man became a living soul.
Amen. Amen.

— James Weldon Johnson

THE CANTICLE OF THE SUN

from: *The Mirror of Perfection*

THIS IS THE PRAISE OF CREATED THINGS, WHICH
HE MADE WHEN THE LORD CERTIFIED HIM OF HIS KINGDOM

. . . .

Be Thou praised, my Lord, with all Thy creatures,
   above all Brother Sun,
   who gives the day and lightens us therewith.

And he is beautiful and radiant with great splendour,
   of Thee, Most High, he bears similitude.

Be Thou praised, my Lord, of Sister Moon and the stars,
   in the heaven hast Thou formed them, clear and precious
      and comely.

Be Thou praised, my Lord, of Brother Wind,
   and of the air, and the cloud, and of fair and of all
      weather,
   by the which Thou givest to Thy creatures sustenance.

Be Thou praised, my Lord, of Sister Water,
   who is very serviceable unto us, and humble and precious
      and clean.

Be Thou praised, my Lord, of Brother Fire,
   by which Thou hast lightened the night,
   and he is beautiful and joyful and robust and strong.

Be Thou praised, my Lord, of our Sister Mother Earth,
   which sustains and hath us in rule,
   and produces divers fruits with coloured flowers and
      herbs.

. . . .

Praise ye and bless my Lord, and give Him thanks,
and serve Him with great humility.

— *Saint Francis of Assisi*

adapted from the translation of *Robert Steele*

THE SHEPHERD

The shepherds sing; and shall I silent be?
My God, no hymne for Thee?
My soul's a shepherd too; a flock it feeds
Of thoughts and words and deeds:
The pasture is Thy word; the streams Thy grace,
Enriching all the place.
Shepherd and flock shall sing, and all my powers
Out-sing the day-light houres.

— *George Herbert*

THE VOICE OF GOD

I bent again unto the ground
And I heard the quiet sound
Which the grasses make when they
Come up laughing from the clay.

— *We are the voice of God!* — they said:
Thereupon I bent my head
Down again that I might see
If they truly spoke to me.

But, around me, everywhere,
Grass and tree and mountain were
Thundering in mighty glee,
— *We are the voice of deity!* —

And I leapt from where I lay:
I danced upon the laughing clay:
And, to the rock that sang beside,
— *We are the voice of God!* — I cried.

— James Stephens

from: PIED BEAUTY

Glory be to God for dappled things —
　　For skies of couple-colour as a brinded cow;
　　　　For rose-moles all in stipple upon trout that **swim**;
Fresh-firecoal chestnut-falls; finches' wings;
　　Landscape plotted and pieced — fold, fallow, and **plough**;
　　And áll trádes, their gear and tackle and trim.

All things counter, original, spare, strange;
　　Whatever is fickle, freckled (who knows how?)
　　　　With swift, slow; sweet, sour; adazzle, dim;
He fathers-forth whose beauty is past change:
　　　　　　Praise him.

— Gerard Manley Hopkins

♪ SAINT PATRICK'S BREASTPLATE

(Also known as 'The Deer's Cry.' This very old rune, which has survived from the Seventh Century, is said to have been spoken by St. Patrick on his way to Tara, to join in combat with the pagan High-King of Ireland. As he chanted the words, assassins lying in ambush ready to kill him and his followers saw only a herd of deer wandering by.)

I arise today
Through the strength of heaven:
Light of sun,
Radiance of moon,
Splendour of fire,
Speed of lightning,
Swiftness of wind,
Depth of sea,
Stability of earth,
Firmness of rock.

I arise today
Through God's strength to pilot me:
God's might to uphold me,
God's wisdom to guide me,
God's eye to look before me,
God's ear to hear me,
God's word to speak for me,
God's hand to guard me,
God's way to lie before me,
God's shield to protect me,
God's hosts to save me
From snares of devils,
From temptations of vices,

♪ The treble clef sign against a title indicates that the poem has been set to music, of which particulars will be found, under the title, in the *Index of Musical Settings* at the end of the book.

From everyone who shall wish me ill,
Afar and anear,
Alone and in a multitude.

Christ to shield me today
Against poison, against burning,
Against drowning, against wounding,
So that there may come to me abundance of reward.
Christ with me, Christ before me, Christ behind me,
Christ in me, Christ beneath me, Christ above me,
Christ on my right, Christ on my left,
Christ when I lie down, Christ when I sit, Christ when
        I arise,
Christ in the heart of every man who thinks of me,
Christ in the mouth of every one who speaks of me,
Christ in every eye that sees me,
Christ in every ear that hears me.

I arise today
Through a mighty strength, the invocation of the
        Trinity,
Through belief in the threeness,
Through the confession of the oneness
Of the Creator of Creation.

—Traditional, from the Gaelic

translated by *Kuno Meyer*

from: PRAYER TO THE DARK BIRD

In beauty happily I walk.
With beauty before me, I walk.
With beauty behind me, I walk.
With beauty below me, I walk.
With beauty above me, I walk.
With beauty all around me, I walk.

It is finished again in beauty,
It is finished in beauty,
It is finished in beauty,
It is finished in beauty.

— *Traditional Navajo Indian*

from: *The Navaho Night Chant*

𝄞 'GOD BE IN MY HEDE'

God be in my hede
And in my understandyng,
God be in myne eyes
And in my lokyng,
God be in my mouth
And in my speakyng,
God be in my harte
And in my thinkyng,
God be at myne end
And in my departyng.

— *Anonymous*

from: *The Sarum Primer*, 1558

♪ 'LET US NOW PRAISE FAMOUS MEN . . .'

Let us now praise famous men, and our fathers that begat us.

The Lord hath wrought great glory by them through his great power from the beginning.

Such as did bear rule in their kingdoms, men renowned for their power, giving counsel by their understanding, and declaring prophecies:

Leaders of the people by their counsels, and by their knowledge of learning meet for the people, wise and eloquent in their instructions.

Such as found out musical tunes, and recited verses in writing:

Rich men furnished with ability, living peaceably in their habitations:

All these were honored in their generations, and were the glory of their times.

There be of them that have left a name behind them, that their praises may be reported.

And some there be that have no memorial; who are perished as though they had never been; and are become as though they had never been born; and their children after them.

But these were merciful men, whose righteousness hath not been forgotten.

. . . .

Their seed standeth fast, and their children for their sakes.

Their seed shall remain forever, and their glory shall not be blotted out.

Their bodies are buried in peace, but their name liveth forevermore.

— The Apocrypha

Ecclesiasticus XLIV: 1-10; 12-14

PEACE

My soul, there is a country
    Far beyond the stars,
Where stands a wingèd sentry
    All skilful in the wars:
There, above noise and danger,
    Sweet Peace sits crown'd with smiles,
And One born in a manger
    Commands the beauteous files.
He is thy gracious Friend,
    And — O my soul, awake! —
Did in pure love descend
    To die here for thy sake.
If thou canst get but thither,
    There grows the flower of Peace,
The Rose that cannot wither,
    Thy fortress, and thy ease.
Leave then thy foolish ranges;
    For none can thee secure
But One who never changes —
    Thy God, thy life, thy cure.

— Henry Vaughan

SONG OF THE DAWN

'In the early days of Canada the canoe train would leave at dawn, as it set out on the long voyage to distant Indian encampments. At that early hour of the day, mist lay, cool and gray, low above the water. The fine particles of moisture would gather on the erect figures of the voyageurs, glistening like dust of pearls on their black beards and shining in their black hair, till it seemed as if the men themselves had become a part of the wilderness. Then a voice from the leading canoe would rise from the silent river, chanting the song of the dawn. Voice after voice would take it up, down the long procession of canoes, until from the last in line the chorus came, halting like an echo, through the quiet air.'

Qui vive!
Who is it cries in the dawn —
Cries when the stars go down?
Who is it comes through the mist —
The mist that is fine like lawn,
The mist like an angel's gown?
Who is it comes in the dawn?
Qui vive! Qui vive! in the dawn.

Qui vive!
Who is it passes us by,
Still in the dawn and the mist?
Tall seigneur of the dawn;
A two-edged sword at his thigh,
A shield of gold at his wrist;
Who is it hurrieth by?
Qui vive! Qui vive! in the dawn.

— Unknown

Note: This is described as 'verses of an old song still preserved,' by Sir Gilbert Parker, who quotes it in *The Trail of the Sword.* No trace of it is found, however, in the archives of the National Museum of Canada; and the foremost authorities on Canadian folk-song consider that it was probably composed by a lyric writer 'in the vein of folk-song.' No one knows exactly who did write it; possibly Sir Gilbert Parker himself.

♪ JERUSALEM

And did those feet in ancient time
   Walk upon England's mountains green?
And was the holy Lamb of God
   On England's pleasant pastures seen?

And did the Countenance Divine
   Shine forth upon our clouded hills?
And was Jerusalem builded here
   Among those dark Satanic mills?

Bring me my bow of burning gold!
   Bring me my arrows of desire!
Bring me my spear: O clouds, unfold!
   Bring me my chariot of fire!

I will not cease from mental fight,
   Nor shall my sword sleep in my hand,
Till we have built Jerusalem
   In England's green and pleasant land.

— William Blake

from: *Milton*

A THANKSGIVING TO GOD FOR HIS HOUSE

Lord, Thou hast given me a cell
　　　Wherein to dwell;
A little house, whose humble roof
　　　Is weatherproof;
Under the spars of which I lie
　　　Both soft and dry.
Where Thou, my chamber for to ward,
　　　Hast set a guard
Of harmless thoughts, to watch and keep
　　　Me while I sleep.
Low is my porch, as is my fate,
　　　Both void of state;
And yet the threshold of my door
　　　Is worn by the poor,
Who hither come, and freely get
　　　Good words or meat.
Like as my parlour, so my hall,
　　　And kitchen small;
A little buttery, and therein
　　　A little bin,
Which keeps my little loaf of bread
　　　Unchipt, unflead.
Some brittle sticks of thorn or brier
　　　Make me a fire,
Close by whose living coals I sit,
　　　And glow like it.
Lord, I confess, too, when I dine
　　　The pulse is Thine,
And all those other bits that be
　　　There placed by Thee.

unflead: free from flies, or fleas.
pulse: beans, peas, and other legumes.

The worts, the purslain, and the mess
        Of watercress,
Which of Thy kindness Thou hast sent;
        And my content
Makes those, and my beloved beet
        To be more sweet.
'Tis Thou that crown'st my glittering hearth
        With guiltless mirth;
And giv'st me wassail bowls to drink,
        Spiced to the brink;
Lord, 'tis Thy plenty-dropping hand
        That sows my land:
And giv'st me, for my bushel sown,
        Twice ten for one;
Thou mak'st my teeming hen to lay
        Her egg each day;
Besides my healthful ewes to bear
        Me twins each year;
The whiles the conduits of my kine
        Run cream, for wine,
All these, and better dost Thou send
        Me, to this end,
That I should render, for my part,
        A thankful heart,
Which, fired with incense, I resign
        As wholly Thine;
But the acceptance, that must be,
        My Christ, by Thee.

— Robert Herrick

worts: herbs.
purslain: leafy plant, used in salads.

PRAYER FOR THIS HOUSE

May nothing evil cross this door,
  And may ill-fortune never pry
About these windows; may the roar
  And rains go by.

Strengthened by faith, the rafters will
  Withstand the battering of the storm.
This hearth, though all the world grow chill,
  Will keep you warm.

Peace shall walk softly through these rooms,
  Touching your lips with holy wine,
Till every casual corner blooms
  Into a shrine.

Laughter shall drown the raucous shout
  And, though the sheltering walls are thin,
May they be strong to keep hate out
  And hold love in.

— Louis Untermeyer

BLESSING OF THE KINDLING

I will kindle my fire this morning
In presence of the holy angels of Heaven,
In presence of Ariel of the loveliest form,
In presence of Uriel of the myriad charms,
Without malice, without jealousy, without envy,
Without fear, without terror of anyone under the sun,
But the Holy Son of God to shield me.
    Without malice, without jealousy, without envy,
    Without fear, without terror of anyone under the sun,
    But the Holy Son of God to shield me.

God, kindle thou in my heart within
A flame of love to my neighbour,
To my foe, to my friend, to my kindred all,
To the brave, to the knave, to the thrall,
O Son of the loveliest Mary,
From the lowliest thing that liveth,
To the Name that is highest of all.
    O Son of the loveliest Mary,
    From the lowliest thing that liveth,
    To the Name that is highest of all.

— Traditional, from the Gaelic

THE RUNE OF THE PEAT FIRE

The first layer of peats is laid
down in the name of the God of Life;
the second in the name of the God of Peace;
and the third in the name of the God of Grace.

The Sacred Three:
To save,
To shield,
To surround,
The hearth,
The house,
The household,
This eve,
This night;
O this eve,
This night,
And every night,
Each single night.
Amen.

— *Traditional, from the Gaelic*

recovered by *Kenneth Macleod*

GRACE FOR LIGHT

When we were little childer we had a quare wee house,
　　Away up in the heather by the head o' Brabla' burn;
The hares we'd see them scootin' and we'd hear the crowin'
　　　　grouse,
　　And when we'd all be in at night ye'd not get room to
　　　　turn.

The youngest two she'd put to bed, their faces to the wall,
　　An' the lave of us could sit aroun', just anywhere we
　　　　might;
Herself 'ud take the rush-dip an' light it for us all,
　　An' *'God be thankèd!'* she would say, — *'now, we have
　　a light.'*

Then we be to quet the laughin' an' pushin' on the floor,
　　An' think on One who callèd us to come and be forgiven;
Himself 'ud put his pipe down, an' say the good word more,
　　*'May the Lamb o' God lead us all to the Light o'
　　Heaven!'*

There's a wheen things that used to be an' now has had
　　　　their day,
　　The nine glens of Antrim can show ye many a sight;
But not the quare wee house where we lived up Brabla' way,
　　Nor a child in all the nine Glens that knows the grace
　　for light.

　　　　　　　　　　　　　　　　　　— *Moira O'Neill*

HOSPITALITY

I saw a stranger yestreen;
I put food in the eating place,
Drink in the drinking place,
Music in the listening place;
And, in the sacred name of the Triune,
He blessed myself and my house,
My cattle and my dear ones.
And the lark said in her song,
    Often, often, often,
Goes the Christ in the stranger's guise;
    Often, often, often,
Goes the Christ in the stranger's guise.

— Traditional, from the Gaelic
recovered by *Kenneth Macleod*

HOLY THURSDAY

'Twas on a Holy Thursday, their innocent faces clean,
The children walking two and two, in red and blue and
    green,
Gray-headed beadles walk'd before, with wands as white
    as snow,
Till into the high dome of Paul's they like Thames waters
    flow.

O what a multitude they seem'd, these flowers of London
    town!
Seated in companies they sit with radiance all their own.
The hum of multitudes was there, but multitudes of lambs,
Thousands of little boys and girls, raising their innocent
    hands.

Now like a mighty wind they raise to Heaven the voice of
    song,
Or like harmonious thunderings the seats of Heaven among.
Beneath them sit the aged men, wise guardians of the poor;
Then cherish pity, lest you drive an angel from the door.

— *William Blake*

A VERY OLD GRACE

Bless these Thy Gifts, most gracious God,
From whom all goodness springs;
Make clean our hearts and feed our souls
With good and joyful things.

— *Traditional: English*

ANOTHER GRACE FOR A CHILD

What God gives, and what we take,
'Tis a gift for Christ His sake:
Be the meal of Beans and Pease
God be thanked for those, and these:
Have we flesh, or have we fish,
All are Fragments from His dish.

— *Robert Herrick*

GRACE BEFORE MEAT

Give us grateful hearts, our Father,
for all thy mercies,
and make us mindful of the needs of others;
through Jesus Christ our Lord.

— The Book of Common Prayer (Family Prayers)

FOR QUIET CONFIDENCE

O God of peace, who hast taught us
that in returning and rest we shall be saved,
in quietness and confidence shall be our strength;
By the might of thy Spirit lift us, we pray thee,
to thy presence,
where we may be still and know that thou art God;
through Jesus Christ our Lord.

— The Book of Common Prayer (Family Prayers)

SAN FRANCISCO

Saint that in gentleness
With the wild creatures there
Walked in the wilderness,
Preaching to wolf and snake
Kindness for Jesus' sake,
And to birds of the air:
Of thy sweet friendliness
Mine be a share!
Let me not heedlessly
Waken to fear of me
Any least thing
That goes with claw or wing,
Squirrel in hollow tree,
Birds in their nest.
Let me not needlessly
Scare the shy waterfowl
From reedy rest.
And if I cannot preach
God's gracious word
To any beast or bird,
May all God's creatures teach
God's ways to me!

— *Mary Austin*

♪ THE LAMB

Little Lamb, who made thee?
  Dost thou know who made thee?
Gave thee life and bid thee feed
By the stream and o'er the mead;
Gave thee clothing of delight,
Softest clothing, woolly, bright;
Gave thee such a tender voice,
Making all the vales rejoice?
  Little Lamb, who made thee?
  Dost thou know who made thee?

Little Lamb, I'll tell thee;
  Little Lamb, I'll tell thee;
He is callèd by thy name,
For He calls Himself a Lamb.
He is meek and he is mild,
He became a little child.
I a child, and thou a lamb,
We are callèd by His name;
  Little Lamb, God bless thee!
  Little Lamb, God bless thee!

— William Blake

'THERE BE FOUR THINGS . . . '

There be four things which are little upon the earth,
but they are exceeding wise:

The ants are a people not strong,
yet they prepare their meat in the summer;

The conies are but a feeble folk,
yet make they their houses in the rocks;

The locusts have no king,
yet go they forth all of them by bands.

The spider taketh hold with her hands,
and is in kings' palaces.

— The Bible

Proverbs XXX: 24-28

CHARM FOR GOING A-HUNTING

O my brothers of the wilderness,
My little brothers,
For my necessities I am about to kill you!
May the Master of Life who made you
In the form of the quarry
That my children may be fed,
Speedily provide you another house;
So there may be peace
Between me and thy spirit.

— Mary Austin

𝄞 LITTLE THINGS

Little things, that run, and quail,
And die, in silence and despair!

Little things, that fight, and fail,
And fall, on sea, and earth, and air!

All trapped and frightened little things,
The mouse, the coney, hear our prayer!

As we forgive those done to us,
— The lamb, the linnet, and the hare —

Forgive us all our trespasses,
Little creatures, everywhere!

— James Stephens

THE LITTLE SPRING FLOWS CLEAR AGAIN

The little spring flows clear again
While I stand close to see
What clouded it. If wings were here
To splash the silver merrily
They flew before I came too near.

And if a fawn had rubbed its nose,
Thrust deep in silver, running cool,
Upon the bottom of the spring,
It heard me wading in the pool
Of shadows where the thrushes sing.

29

The little spring flows clear again,
But now is clouded in my mind
The flight of wings that went away —
And something that I came to find
Was loveliness afraid to stay.

— Glenn Ward Dresbach

THE THRUSH'S NEST

Within a thick and spreading hawthorn bush,
    That overhung a molehill large and round,
I heard from morn to morn a merry thrush
    Sing hymns to sunrise, and I drank the sound
With joy; and often, an intruding guest,
    I watched her secret toil from day to day —
How true she warped the moss, to form a nest,
    And modelled it within with wood and clay;
And by-and-by, like heath-bells gilt with dew,
    There lay her shining eggs, as bright as flowers,
Ink-spotted over shells of greeny blue;
    And there I witnessed in the sunny hours,
A brood of Nature's minstrels chirp and fly,
Glad as the sunshine and the laughing sky.

— John Clare

THE FIFTEEN ACRES

I

I cling and swing
On a branch, or sing
Through the cool clear hush of morning O!

Or fling my wing
On the air, and bring
To sleepier birds a warning O!

That the night's in flight!
And the sun's in sight!
And the dew is the grass adorning O!

And the green leaves swing
As I sing, sing, sing:
Up by the river,
Down the dell,
To the little wee nest,
Where the big tree fell,
So early in the morning O!

II

I flit and twit
In the sun for a bit,
When his light so bright is shining O!

Or sit and fit
My plumes, or knit
Straw plaits for the nest's nice lining O!

And she, with glee,
Shows unto me,
Underneath her wing reclining O!

And I sing that Peg
Has an egg, egg, egg!
Up by the oat-field,
Round the mill;
Past the meadow,
Down the hill;
So early in the morning O!

III

I stoop and swoop
On the air, or loop
Through the trees, and then go soaring O!

To group, with a troop,
On the skiey poop,
While the wind behind is roaring O!

I skim and swim
By a cloud's red rim;
And up to the azure flooring O!

And my wide wings drip,
As I slip, slip, slip,
Down through the rain-drops,
Back where Peg
Broods in the nest
On the little white egg,
So early in the morning O!

— James Stephens

THE RIVALS

I heard a bird at dawn
Singing sweetly on a tree,
That the dew was on the lawn,
And the wind was on the lea;
But I didn't listen to him,
For he didn't sing to me!

I didn't listen to him,
For he didn't sing to me
That the dew was on the lawn,
And the wind was on the lea!
I was singing at the time,
Just as prettily as he!

I was singing all the time,
Just as prettily as he,
About the dew upon the lawn,
And the wind upon the lea!
So I didn't listen to him,
As he sang upon a tree!

— *James Stephens*

THE BLACKBIRD

In the far corner,
close by the swings,
every morning
a blackbird sings.

His bill's so yellow
his coat's so black,
that he makes a fellow
whistle back.

Ann, my daughter,
thinks that he
sings for us two
especially.

— *Humbert Wolfe*

NUMBER SONG

Sixteen pigeons flew over the spire
Of the church, and as they went higher
    and higher

They gathered in to be twelve, and ten,
And then they were seven, and then,

When I saw them last they were four —
Wings going, and then nothing more.

— *Elizabeth Madox Roberts*

DUCKS

From troubles of the world
I turn to ducks,
Beautiful comical things
Sleeping or curled
Their heads beneath white wings
By water cool,
Or finding curious things
To eat in various mucks
Beneath the pool,
Tails uppermost, or waddling
Sailor-like on the shores
Of ponds, or paddling
— Left! right! — with fanlike feet
Which are for steady oars
When they (white galleys) float
Each bird a boat
Rippling at will the sweet
Wide waterway . . .
When night is fallen *you* creep
Upstairs, but drakes and dillies
Nest with pale water-stars,
Moonbeams and shadow bars,
And water-lilies:
Fearful too much to sleep
Since they've no locks
To click against the teeth
Of weasel and fox.
And warm beneath
Are eggs of cloudy green
Whence hungry rats and lean

Would stealthily suck
New life, but for the mien,
The bold ferocious mien,
Of the mother-duck.

II

Yes, ducks are valiant things
On nests of twigs and straws,
And ducks are soothy things
And lovely on the lake
When that the sunlight draws
Thereon their pictures dim
In colours cool.
And when beneath the pool
They dabble, and when they swim
And make their rippling rings,
O ducks are beautiful things!
But ducks are comical things: —
As comical as you.
Quack!
They waddle round, they do.
They eat all sorts of things,
And then they quack.
By barn and stable and stack
They wander at their will,
But if you go too near
They look at you through black
Small topaz-tinted eyes
And wish you ill.
Triangular and clear
They leave their curious track
In mud at the water's edge,
And there amid the sedge

And slime they gobble and peer
Saying 'Quack! quack!'

III

When God had finished the stars and whirl of coloured suns
He turned His mind from big things to fashion little ones;
Beautiful tiny things (like daisies) He made, and then
He made the comical ones in case the minds of men
        Should stiffen and become
        Dull, humourless and glum,
And so forgetful of their Maker be
As to take even themselves — *quite seriously*.
Caterpillars and cats are lively and excellent puns:
All God's jokes are good — even the practical ones!
And as for the duck, I think God must have smiled a bit
Seeing those bright eyes blink on the day He fashioned it.
And He's probably laughing still at the sound that came
    out of its bill!

                         — *F. W. Harvey*

DUCKS' DITTY

All along the backwater,
Through the rushes tall,
Ducks are a-dabbling,
Up tails all!

Ducks' tails, drakes' tails,
Yellow feet a-quiver,
Yellow bills all out of sight
Busy in the river!

Slushy green undergrowth
Where the roach swim —
Here we keep our larder,
Cool and full and dim.

Every one for what he likes!
We like to be
Heads down, tails up,
Dabbling free!

High in the blue above
Swifts whirl and call —
We are down a-dabbling
Up tails all!

— *Kenneth Grahame*

LITTLE TROTTY WAGTAIL

Little trotty wagtail, he went in the rain,
And twittering, tottering sideways he ne'er got straight
    again.
He stooped to get a worm, and looked up to get a fly,
And then he flew away ere his feathers they were dry.

Little trotty wagtail, he waddled in the mud,
And left his little footmarks, trample where he would;
He waddled in the water-pudge, and waggle went his tail,
And chirrupt up his wings to dry upon the garden rail.

Little trotty wagtail, you nimble all about,
And in the dimpling water-pudge you waddle in and out;
Your home is nigh at hand, and in the warm pig-stye,
So, little Master Wagtail, I'll bid you good-bye.

— *John Clare*

from: I STOOD TIP-TOE UPON A LITTLE HILL

. . . Swarms of minnows show their little heads,
Staying their wavy bodies 'gainst the streams,
To taste the luxury of sunny beams
Tempered with coolness. How they ever wrestle
With their own sweet delight, and ever nestle
Their silver bellies on the pebbly sand.
If you but scantily hold out the hand,
That very instant not one will remain;
But turn your eye, and they are there again.
The ripples seem right glad to reach those cresses,
And cool themselves among the em'rald tresses;
The while they cool themselves, they freshness give,
And moisture, that the bowery green may live.

— John Keats

THE SILENT SNAKE

The birds go fluttering in the air,
   The rabbits run and skip,
Brown squirrels race along the bough,
   The May-flies rise and dip;
But, whilst these creatures play and leap,
The silent snake goes *creepy-creep!*

The birdies sing and whistle loud,
   The busy insects hum,
The squirrels chat, the frogs say 'Croak!'
   But the snake is always dumb.
With not a sound through grasses deep
The silent snake goes *creepy-creep!*

— Anonymous

THE HOUSEKEEPER

The frugal snail, with forecast of repose,
Carries his house with him wher'er he goes;
Peeps out, — and if there comes a shower of rain,
Retreats to his small domicile again.
Touch but a tip of him, a horn, — 'tis well, —
He curls up in his sanctuary shell.
He's his own landlord, his own tenant; stay
Long as he will, he dreads no quarter day.
Himself he boards and lodges; both invites
And feasts himself; sleeps with himself o' nights.
He spares the upholsterer trouble to procure
Chattels; himself is his own furniture,
And his sole riches. Wheresoe'er he roam, —
Knock when you will, — he's sure to be at home.

— *Charles Lamb*

... Therefore doth heaven divide
The state of man in divers functions,
Setting endeavour in continual motion;
To which is fixed, as an aim or butt,
Obedience: for so work the honey-bees,
Creatures that by a rule in nature teach
The act of order to a peopled kingdom.
They have a king and officers of sorts;
Where some, like magistrates, correct at home,
Others, like merchants, venture trade abroad,
Others, like soldiers, armed in their stings,
Make boot upon the summer's velvet buds,
Which pillage they with merry march bring home
To the tent-royal of their emperor;
Who, busied in his majesty, surveys
The singing masons building roofs of gold,
The civil citizens kneading up the honey,
The poor mechanic porters crowding in
Their heavy burdens at his narrow gate,
The sad-eyed justice, with his surly hum,
Delivering o'er to executors pale
The lazy yawning drone.

— *William Shakespeare*

from: *Henry V:* Act I. Scene 2

THE FIELD MOUSE

When the moon shines o'er the corn
And the beetle drones his horn,
And the flittermice swift fly,
And the nightjars swooping cry,
And the young hares run and leap,
We waken from our sleep.

And we climb with tiny feet
And we munch the green corn sweet
With startled eyes for fear
The white owl should fly near,
Or long slim weasel spring
Upon us where we swing.

We do no hurt at all;
Is there not room for all
Within the happy world?
All day we lie close curled
In drowsy sleep, nor rise
Till through the dusky skies
The moon shines o'er the corn
And the beetle drones his horn.

— *Fiona Macleod (William Sharp)*

THE MOUSE

I hear a mouse
Bitterly complaining
In a crack of moonlight
Aslant on the floor —

'Little I ask
And that little is not granted.
There are few crumbs
In this world any more.

'The breadbox is tin
And I cannot get in.

'The jam's in a jar
My teeth cannot mar.

'The cheese sits by itself
On the pantry shelf.

'All night I run
Searching and seeking.
All night I run
About on the floor.

'Moonlight is there
And a bare place for dancing,
But no little feast
Is spread any more.'

— Elizabeth Coatsworth

ON A CAT, AGEING

He blinks upon the hearth-rug
And yawns in deep content,
Accepting all the comforts
That Providence has sent.

Louder he purrs, and louder,
In one glad hymn of praise
For all the night's adventures,
For quiet, restful days.

Life will go on forever,
With all that cat can wish;
Warmth, and the glad procession
Of fish and milk and fish.

Only — the thought disturbs him —
He's noticed once or twice,
That times are somehow breeding
A nimbler race of mice.

— Alexander Gray

44

MILK FOR THE CAT

When the tea is brought at five o'clock,
   And all the neat curtains are drawn with care,
The little black cat with bright green eyes
   Is suddenly purring there.

At first she pretends, having nothing to do,
   She has come in merely to blink by the grate,
But, though tea may be late or the milk be sour,
   She is never late.

And presently her agate eyes
   Take a soft large milky haze,
And her independent casual glance
   Becomes a stiff hard gaze.

Then she stamps her claws or lifts her ears
   Or twists her tail or begins to stir,
Till suddenly all her lithe body becomes
   One breathing trembling purr.

The children eat and wriggle and laugh;
   The two old ladies stroke their silk:
But the cat is grown small and thin with desire,
   Transformed to a creeping lust for milk.

The white saucer like some full moon descends
   At last from the clouds of the table above;
She sighs and dreams and thrills and glows,
   Transfigured with love.

She nestles over the shining rim,
   Buries her chin in the creamy sea;

Her tail hangs loose; each drowsy paw
　　Is doubled under each bending knee.

A long, dim ecstasy holds her life;
　　Her world is an infinite shapeless white,
Till her tongue has curled the last holy drop,
　　Then she sinks back into the night,

Draws and dips her body to heap
　　Her sleepy nerves in the great arm-chair,
Lies defeated and buried deep
　　Three or four hours unconscious there.

— Harold Monro

EPITAPH FOR A PERSIAN KITTEN

Death, who one day taketh all,
Wise or good or great or small,
Every creature of the air,
Every creature of the sea,
All life here and everywhere,
What is thine we give to thee.
Neither great nor very wise,
Yet belovèd in our eyes,
Lightly hold, and gently keep
A small, good kitten in her sleep.

— Miriam Vedder

SEAL LULLABY

Oh! hush thee, my baby, the night is behind us,
  And black are the waters that sparkled so green.
The moon, o'er the combers, looks downward to find us
  At rest in the hollows that rustle between.
Where billow meets billow, there soft be thy pillow;
  Ah, weary wee flipperling, curl at thy ease!
The storm shall not wake thee, nor shark overtake thee,
  Asleep in the arms of the slow-swinging seas.

— Rudyard Kipling

THE BROWN BEAR

Now the wild bees that hive in the rocks
Are winding their horns, elfin shrill,
And hark, at the pine tree the woodpecker knocks,
And the speckled grouse pipes on the hill.
Now the adder's dull brood wakes to run,
Now the sap mounts abundant and good,
And the brown bear has turned with his side to the sun
In his lair in the depth of the wood —
Old Honey-Paw wakes in the wood.

'Oh, a little more slumber,' says he,
'And a little more turning to sleep,'
But he feels the spring fervor that hurries the bee
And the hunger that makes the trout leap;
So he ambles by thicket and trail,
So he noses the tender young shoots,
In the spring of the year at the sign of the quail
The brown bear goes digging for roots —
For sappy and succulent roots.

47

Oh, as still goes the wolf on his quest
As the spotted snake glides through the rocks,
And the deer and the sheep count the lightest foot best,
And slinking and sly trots the fox.
But fleet-foot and light-foot will stay,
And fawns by their mothers will quail
At the saplings that snap and the thickets that sway
When Honey-Paw takes to the trail —
When he shuffles and grunts on the trail.

He has gathered the ground squirrel's hoard,
He has rifled the store of the bees,
He has caught the young trout at the shoals of the ford
And stripped the wild plums from the trees;
So robbing and raging he goes,
And the right to his pillage makes good
Till he rounds out the year at the first of the snows
In his lair in the depth of the wood —
Old Honey-Paw sleeps in the wood.

— Mary Austin

NOSEGAY FOR A YOUNG GOAT

With what smug elegance the small goat minces
    Over the rocks to me; inquisitive,
Yet quite sedate, he fearlessly evinces
    Interest in what my outstretched hand may give.

His horns are dainty curves, his beard points trimly;
    He has an eye that's both demure and shrewd.
And yet for all he moves his lips so primly,
    Spoken aloud, his language might be lewd.

It makes me smile to see so much that's charming,
   So grave, naïve, and innocent a grace,
An air so decorous and so disarming,
   Combined with that uncouth and crafty face.

— Winifred Welles

ROAD-SONG OF THE BANDAR LOG

Here we go in a flung festoon,
Half-way up to the jealous moon!
Don't you envy our pranceful bands?
Don't you wish you had extra hands?
Wouldn't you like if your tails were — *so* —
Curved in the shape of a Cupid's bow?
   Now you're angry, but — never mind,
   Brother, thy tail hangs down behind!

Here we sit in a branchy row,
Thinking of beautiful things we know;
Dreaming of deeds that we mean to do,
All complete, in a minute or two —
Something noble and grand and good,
Won by merely wishing we could.
   Now we're going to — never mind,
   Brother, thy tail hangs down behind!

All the talk we ever have heard
Uttered by bat or beast or bird —
Hide or fin or scale or feather —
Jabber it quickly and all together!
Excellent! Wonderful! Once again!
Now we are talking just like men.

49

Let's pretend we are . . . never mind,
Brother, thy tail hangs down behind!
This is the way of the Monkey-kind.

Then join our leaping lines that scumfish through the pines,
That rocket by where, light and high, the wild-grape swings.
By the rubbish in our wake, and the noble noise we make,
Be sure, be sure, we're going to do some splendid things.

— *Rudyard Kipling*

SONG OF THE DOG 'QUOODLE'

They haven't got no noses,
   The fallen sons of Eve;
Even the smell of roses
Is not what they supposes,
But more than mind discloses
   And more than men believe.

The brilliant smell of water,
   The brave smell of a stone,
The smell of dew and thunder,
The old bones buried under,
Are things in which they blunder
   And err, if left alone.

The wind from winter forests,
   The scent of scentless flowers,
The breath of bride's adorning,
The smell of snare and warning,
The smell of Sunday morning,
   God gave to us for ours.

And Quoodle here discloses
　　All things that Quoodle can,
They haven't got no noses,
They haven't got no noses,
And goodness only knowses
　　The Noselessness of Man.

— Gilbert Keith Chesterton

CONNECTICUT RONDEL

He shakes his mane upon the breeze
And gallops through the grasses;
He does not like the encircling trees —
He likes to see what passes.

He trots along much at his ease
And snatches as he passes,
Then shakes his mane upon the breeze
And gallops through the grasses.

He does not like the buzz of bees
That fades and then repasses;
He loves the open swish of trees
And the wide hum of grasses:
He shakes his mane upon the breeze.

— Marion Canby

THE RUNAWAY

Once when the snow of the year was beginning to fall,
We stopped by a mountain pasture to say, 'Whose colt?'
A little Morgan had one forefoot on the wall,
The other curled at his breast. He dipped his head
And snorted at us. And then he had to bolt.
We heard the miniature thunder where he fled,
And we saw him, or thought we saw him, dim and grey,
Like a shadow against the curtain of falling flakes.
'I think the little fellow's afraid of the snow.
He isn't winter-broken. It isn't play
With the little fellow at all. He's running away.'
I doubt if even his mother could tell him, 'Sakes,
It's only weather.' He'd think she didn't know!
'Where is his mother? He can't be out alone.'
And now he comes again with clatter of stone,
And mounts the wall again with whited eyes
And all his tail that isn't hair up straight.
He shudders his coat as if to throw off flies.
'Whoever it is that leaves him out so late,
When other creatures have gone to stall and bin,
Ought to be told to come and take him in.'

— Robert Frost

HIGHLAND FAIRIES

(Being some experiences of a child sent for the body's sake
to a shooting-lodge in the hills to the care of a stalker and his
wife.)

I showed Donald the pictures in my picture-book
Of fairies in the moonlight dancing round about a tree.
I told Donald that I was fond of fairies,
And Donald smiled so far-away and took me on his knee.
One morning very early while still the sun was yawning,
Mairi came and dressed me and gave me milk and bread;
And I set out with Donald and the little baby morning;
'We'll go and see the fairies now,' was all that Donald said.
So up the hill and up the hill I went on Donald's garron
(That's what he calls his pony. I call it Dapple-grey).

Then Donald whispered: 'Quiet, now! We're very near the
    fairies.'
And creepy-creep we clambered up, and peeped above the
    brae.
There were all the fairies in funny coats of brown and
    white,
Dancing, dancing, dancing on the grass where dew-drops
    shone.
Flash, flash went their feet. Their mothers all stood watch-
    ing.
And Donald clapped his hands, and wheef! the fairies were
    all gone.
These fairies' names are Laoigh. They come into the world
    in June,
And dance and dance upon the hills among the heather
    wild.
I used to want to be a fairy like they are in picture-books,
But now I'm all for Laoigh — the red deer child.

54

I told Donald a story about fairies
That flew on wings across the world, and Donald smiled
    and said:
'I would be a-takin' you to see the flying fairies,
If Mairi mightn't be too sure that it was time for bed!'
So I kissed Mairi, and went away with Donald then
In the winter evening dark among the frost and snow,
I on Donald's shoulder wrapped up in a tartan plaid
That grew on Donald's father's sheep a hundred years ago.
And when we came at last away up on the mountain
Where the stars were sharp as knives, Donald whispered:
    'There!'
And I saw the fairies with white wings of gossamer
Flying in the starlight through the shadows of the air.
All white and silent went the flying hill-top fairies.
From the snow into the mist their flitting dance began.
I asked Donald, were they sprites or gnomes or elfin-folk?
And Donald told me that the fairies' name was Ptarmigan.

The brown burn's a gnome that was born in a cavern,
The brown thrush a kindly elf that loves to sing to me,
And the wind among the grasses is a little goblin fellow
That plays the strangest sort of games around the rowan
    tree.
So I forgot my picture-book with all its kind of fairies —
The Fairy Queens in party frocks with starch in every frill.
And I find all my fairies now in my dear Donald's picture-
    book —
That very splendid picture-book that Donald calls a hill.

— *J. B. Salmond*

ptarmigan: a bird of the grouse family, of a white color in winter, frequenting the summits of European mountains.
  burn: a brook.

55

THE LEPRACAUN or THE FAIRY SHOEMAKER

Little Cowboy, what have you heard,
　　Up on the lonely rath's green mound?
Only the plaintive yellow bird
　　Sighing in sultry fields around,
Chary, chary, chary, chee-ee! —
Only the grasshopper and the bee? —
　　　　'Tip-tap, rip-rap,
　　　　Tick-a-tack-too!
　　Scarlet leather, sewn together,
　　　　This will make a shoe.
　　Left, right, pull it tight;
　　　　Summer days are warm;
　　Underground in winter,
　　　　Laughing at the storm!'
Lay your ear close to the hill.
　　Do you not catch the tiny clamour,
　　Busy click of an elfin hammer,
Voice of the Lepracaun singing shrill
　　As he merrily plies his trade?
　　　　He's a span
　　　　And a quarter in height.
Get him in sight, hold him tight,
　　　　And you're a made
　　　　　　Man!

You watch your cattle the summer day,
　　Sup on potatoes, sleep in the hay;
How would you like to roll in your carriage,
Look for a duchess's daughter in marriage?
　　Seize the Shoe-maker — then you may!
　　　　'Big boots a-hunting,
　　　　Sandals in the hall,

White for a wedding-feast,
   Pink for a ball.
This way, that way,
   So we make a shoe;
Getting rich every stitch,
   Tick-tack-too!'
Nine-and-ninety treasure-crocks
  This keen miser-fairy hath,
Hid in mountains, woods and rocks,
  Ruin and round-tow'r, cave and rath,
And where the cormorants build;
   From times of old
   Guarded by him;
   Each of them fill'd
   Full to the brim
     With gold!

I caught him at work one day, myself,
  In the castle-ditch, where foxglove grows;
A wrinkled, wizen'd, and bearded Elf,
  Spectacles stuck on his pointed nose,
  Silver buckles to his hose,
Leather apron — shoe in his lap —
   'Rip-rap, tip-tap,
   Tick-tack-too!
  (A grasshopper on my cap!
   Away the moth flew!)
  Buskins for a fairy prince,
   Brogues for his son —
  Pay me well, pay me well
   When the job is done!'
The rogue was mine, beyond a doubt.
  I stared at him; he stared at me;
  'Servant, Sir!' 'Humph!' says he,

And pulled a snuff-box out.
He took a long pinch, look'd better pleased,
    The queer little Lepracaun;
Offered the box with a whimsical grace —
Pouf! he flung the dust in my face,
        And, while I sneezed,
            Was gone!

— *William Allingham*

FOR A MOCKING VOICE

Who calls? Who calls? Who?
Did you call? Did you? —
I call! I call! I!
Follow where I fly. —
Where? O where? O where?
On Earth or in the Air? —
Where you come, I'm gone!
Where you fly, I've flown! —
Stay! ah, stay! ah, stay,
Pretty Elf, and play!
Tell me where you are —
Ha, ha, ha, ha, ha!

— *Eleanor Farjeon*

♩ 'OVER HILL, OVER DALE'

(Puck: How now, spirit! Whither wander you?)

The Fairy: Over hill, over dale,
       Through bush, through brier,
       Over park, over pale,
       Through flood, through fire!
     I do wander everywhere,
     Swifter than the moon's sphere;
     And I serve the fairy queen,
     To dew her orbs upon the green:
     The cowslips tall her pensioners be;
     In their gold coats spots you see;
     Those be rubies, fairy favours,
     In those freckles live their savours:
   I must go seek some dew-drops here,
   And hang a pearl in every cowslip's ear.
   Farewell, thou lob of spirits, I'll be gone!
   Our queen and all her elves come here anon.

— William Shakespeare

from: *A Midsummer Night's Dream,* Act II, Scene 1

from: OBERON'S FEAST

A little mushroom table spread,
After short prayers, they set on bread;
A moon-parch'd grain of purest wheat,
With some small glitt'ring grit, to eat
His choice bits with; then in a trice
They make a feast less great than nice.
But all this while his eye is serv'd,
We must not think his ear was starv'd:
But that there was in place to stir
His spleen, the chirring grasshopper;
The merry cricket, the puling fly,
The piping gnat for minstrelsy.
And now, we must imagine first,
The elves present to quench his thirst
A pure seed-pearl of infant dew,
Brought and besweetened in a blue
And pregnant violet; which done,
His kitling eyes begin to run
Quite through the table, where he spys
The horns of papery butterflies,
Of which he eats, and tastes a little
Of what we call the Cuckoo's spittle.
A little fuzz-ball pudding stands
By, yet not blessed by his hands
That was too coarse; but then forthwith
He ventures boldly on the pith
Of sugared rush, and eats the sag
And well bestrutted bee's sweet bag:
Gladding his palate with some store
Of emmit's eggs: what would he more?

— Robert Herrick

'QUEEN MAB'

This is Mab, the mistress fairy,
That doth nightly rob the dairy,
And can hurt or help the churning
(As she please) without discerning.
She that pinches country wenches,
If they rub not clean their benches,
And with sharper nails remembers
When they rake not up their embers.
But, if so they chance to feast her,
In a shoe she drops a tester.

— *Ben Jonson*

from: *The Satyr*

'THROUGH THE HOUSE GIVE GLIMMERING LIGHT'

Through the house give glimmering light,
  By the dead and drowsy fire:
Every elf and fairy sprite
  Hop as light as bird from brier;
And this ditty, after me,
Sing, and dance it trippingly.

First, rehearse your song by rote,
To each word a warbling note:
Hand in hand, with fairy grace,
Will we sing, and bless this place.

— *William Shakespeare*

from: *A Midsummer Night's Dream*, Act V, Scene 2

61

'QUEEN MAB'

O then, I see, Queen Mab hath been with you.
She is the fairies' midwife, and she comes
In shape no bigger than an agate-stone
On the forefinger of an alderman,
Drawn with a team of little atomies
Athwart men's noses as they lie asleep:
Her wagon-spokes made of long spinners' legs;
The cover, of the wings of grasshoppers;
The traces, of the smallest spider's web;
The collars, of the moonshine's watery beams;
Her whip of cricket's bone; the lash, of film;
Her wagoner, a small grey-coated gnat,
Not half so big as a round little worm
Pricked from the lazy finger of a maid:
Her chariot is an empty hazel-nut,
Made by the joiner squirrel, or old grub,
Time out o' mind the fairies' coachmakers.
And in this state she gallops night by night
Through lovers' brains, and then they dream of love;
O'er courtiers' knees, that dream on court'sies straight;
O'er lawyers' fingers, who straight dream on fees;
O'er ladies' lips, who straight on kisses dream.

— *William Shakespeare*

from: *Romeo and Juliet,* Act I, Scene 4

By the moon we sport and play,
With the night begins our day:
As we dance the dew doth fall,
Trip it little urchins all:
Lightly as the little Bee,
Two by two and three by three:
And about go we, and about go we.

I do come about the copse,
Leaping upon flower tops:
Then I get upon a fly,
She carries me above the sky:
And trip and go.

When a dew drop falleth down,
And doth light upon my crown,
Then I shake my head and skip,
And about I trip.
Two by two and three by three:
And about go we, and about go we.

— *John Lyly*

from: *The Maydes' Metamorphosis*

THE STOLEN PRINCESS

O scented ropes in the forest catch at her little feet,
    Honeysuckle and woodbine, binding her down and
        down,
While over her head the oak-tree's star-shotten branches
    meet
    And foxgloves nod in the bracken, pink as her own pink
        gown.
There in the leafy silence, there in the heart o' the dell
    The Wee Folk and the Good Folk hold her for ever and
        a day,
And down in the oak-tree forest only the lark can tell
    How she was stol'n by the fairies in the pride o' the May.

O ankle deep in the daisies she stands from dawn till dawn.
    The half-blown roses open and the full-blown roses fall,
While summer and winter tiptoe over the forest lawn
    And saplings rise from the acorns, mistily green and tall.
Soon she will be but a foxglove where other foxgloves grow,
    Down in the oak-tree hollow with woodbine barring the
        way,
Pink-gowned there in the dimness with only the lark to
    know
    How she was stol'n by the fairies in the pride o' the May.

— Joan Noble MacKenzie

OVERHEARD ON A SALTMARSH

Nymph, nymph, what are your beads?

    Green glass, goblin. Why do you stare at them?

Give them me.

      No.

Give them me. Give them me.

          No.

Then I will howl all night in the reeds,
Lie in the mud and howl for them.

Goblin, why do you love them so?

They are better than stars or water,
Better than voices of winds that sing,
Better than any man's fair daughter,
Your green glass beads on a silver ring.

Hush, I stole them out of the moon.

Give me your beads, I desire them.

          No.

I will howl in a deep lagoon
For your green glass beads, I love them so.
Give them me. Give them.

          No.

          — *Harold Monro*

GOBLIN FEET

I am off down the road
Where the fairy lanterns glowed
And the little pretty flitter-mice are flying:
A slender band of gray
It runs creepily away
And the hedges and the grasses are a-sighing.
The air is full of wings,
And of blundery beetle-things
That warn you with their whirring and their humming.
O! I hear the tiny horns
Of enchanted leprechauns
And the padded feet of many gnomes a-coming!

O! the lights! O! the gleams! O! the little tinkly sounds!
O! the rustle of their noiseless little robes!
O! the echo of their feet — of their happy little feet!
O! their swinging lamps in little starlit globes.

I must follow in their train
Down the crooked fairy lane
Where the coney-rabbits long ago have gone,
And where silvery they sing
In a moving moonlit ring
All a-twinkle with the jewels they have on.
They are fading round the turn
Where the glow-worms palely burn
And the echo of their padding feet is dying!
O! it's knocking at my heart —
Let me go! O! let me start!
For the little magic hours are all a-flying.

O! the warmth! O! the hum! O! the colours in the dark!
O! the gauzy wings of golden honey-flies!
O! the music of their feet — of their dancing goblin feet!
O! the magic! O! the sorrow when it dies.

— *J. R. R. Tolkien*

THE SONG OF WANDERING AENGUS

I went out to the hazel wood
Because a fire was in my head,
And cut and peeled a hazel wand,
And hooked a berry to a thread;
And when white moths were on the wing,
And moth-like stars were flickering out,
I dropped the berry in a stream,
And caught a little silver trout.

When I had laid it on the floor,
I went to blow the fire a-flame,
But something rustled on the floor,
And someone called me by my name:
It had become a glimmering girl
With apple blossom in her hair
Who called me by my name and ran
And faded through the brightening air.

Though I am old with wandering
Through hollow lands and hilly lands,
I will find out where she has gone,
And kiss her lips and take her hands;
And walk among long dappled grass,
And pluck till time and times are done
The silver apples of the moon,
The golden apples of the sun.

— *William Butler Yeats*

THE LONELY HOUSE

I know some lonely houses off the road
A robber'd like the look of, —
Wooden barred,
And windows hanging low,
Inviting to
A portico,
Where two could creep:
One hand the tools,
The other peep
To make sure all's asleep.
Old-fashioned eyes,
Not easy to surprise!

How orderly the kitchen'd look by night,
With just a clock, —
But they could gag the tick,
And mice won't bark.
And so the walls don't tell,
None will.

A pair of spectacles ajar just stir —
An almanac's aware.
Was it the mat winked,
Or a nervous star?
The moon slides down the stair
To see who's there.

There's plunder, — where?
Tankard, or spoon,
Earring, or stone,
A watch, some ancient brooch
To match the grandmamma,
Staid sleeping there.

Day rattles, too,
Stealth's slow;
The sun has got as far
As the third sycamore.
Screams chanticleer,
'Who's there?'
And echoes, trains away,
Sneer — 'Where?'
While the old couple, just astir,
Fancy the sunrise left the door ajar!

— Emily Dickinson

THE HARE

In the black furrow of a field
I saw an old witch-hare this night;
And she cocked a lissome ear,
And she eyed the moon so bright,
And she nibbled o' the green;
And I whispered 'Whsst! witch-hare,'
Away like a ghostie o'er the field
She fled, and left the moonlight there.

— Walter de la Mare

I SAW THREE WITCHES

I saw three witches
That bowed down like barley,
And straddled their brooms 'neath a louring sky,
And, mounting a storm-cloud,
Aloft on its margin,
Stood black in the silver as up they did fly.

I saw three witches
That mocked the poor sparrows
They carried in cages of wicker along,
Till a hawk from his eyrie
Swooped down like an arrow,
Smote on the cages, and ended their song.

I saw three witches
That sailed in a shallop,
All turning their heads with a smickering smile,
Till a bank of green osiers
Concealed their grim faces,
Though I heard them lamenting for many a mile.

I saw three witches
Asleep in a valley,
Their heads in a row, like stones in a flood,
Till the moon, creeping upward,
Looked white through the valley,
And turned them to bushes in bright scarlet bud.

— Walter de la Mare

'THE WITCHES' SPELL'

Thrice the brinded cat hath mew'd.
  Thrice, and once the hedge-pig whin'd.
Harpier cries: — 'Tis time, 'tis time.
Round about the cauldron go;
In the poison'd entrails throw.
Toad, that under coldest stone,
Days and nights hast thirty-one
Swelter'd venom sleeping got,
Boil thou first i' the charmed pot!
  Double, double, toil and trouble;
  Fire, burn; and, cauldron, bubble;
Fillet of a fenny snake,
In the cauldron boil and bake:
Eye of newt, and toe of frog,
Wool of bat, and tongue of dog,
Adder's fork, and blind-worm's sting,
Lizard's leg and owlet's wing,
For a charm of powerful trouble;
Like a hell-broth boil and bubble.
  Double, double, toil and trouble;
  Fire, burn; and, cauldron, bubble.
Scale of dragon, tooth of wolf;
Witches' mummy; maw, and gulf,
Of the ravin'd salt-sea shark;
Root of hemlock, digg'd i' the dark;
Liver of blaspheming Jew;
Gall of goat, and slips of yew
Sliver'd in the moon's eclipse;
Nose of Turk, and Tartar's lips;
Finger of birth-strangled babe,
Ditch-deliver'd by a drab,
Make the gruel thick and slab;

Add thereto a tiger's chaudron,
For the ingredients of our cauldron.
　　Double, double, toil and trouble;
　　Fire, burn; and, cauldron, bubble.
Cool it with a baboon's blood,
Then the charm is firm and good.

— William Shakespeare

from: *Macbeth,* Act IV, Scene 1

'THE CAT SITS AT THE MILL DOOR . . .'

The cat sits at the mill door spinnin', spinnin'.
Up comes a wee mouse rinnin', rinnin'.
'What are ye doin' there, my lady, my lady?'
'Spinnin' a sark for my son,' quo' Batty, quo' Batty.
'I'll tell a story, my lady, my lady,'
'We'll hae the mair company,' quo' Batty, quo' Batty.
'There was once a wee woman, my lady, my lady.'
'She tuk the less room,' quo' Batty, quo' Batty.
'She was sweepin' her house one day, my lady, my lady,'
'She had it the cleaner,' quo' Batty, quo' Batty.
'She found a penny, my lady, my lady.'
'She had the mair money,' quo' Batty, quo' Batty.
'She went to the market, my lady, my lady,'
'She didna stay at hame,' quo' Batty, quo' Batty.
'She bocht a wee bit o' beef, my lady, my lady.'
'She had the mair flesh meat,' quo' Batty, quo' Batty.
'She cam' home, my lady, my lady.'
'She didna stay awa',' quo' Batty, quo' Batty.
'She put her beef on the coals to roast, my lady, my lady.'
'She didna eat it raw,' quo' Batty, quo' Batty.
'She put it on the window to cool, my lady, my lady.'
'She didna scaud her lips,' quo' Batty, quo' Batty.
'Up comes a wee mouse an' ate it all up, my lady, my lady.'
'Ay, and that's the way I'll eat *you* up too,' quo' Batty, quo'
    Batty,
        Quo' *Batty,* quo' *BATTY,*
        Quo' BATTY.

                   — *Traditional: Scots*

EEKA, NEEKA

Eeka, Neeka, Leeka, Lee —
Here's a lock without a key;
Bring a lantern, bring a candle,
Here's a door without a handle;
Shine, shine, you old thief Moon,
Here's a door without a room;
Not a whisper, moth or mouse,
Here's a room without a house!

Say nothing, creep away,
And live to knock another day!

— *Walter de la Mare*

COUNTING-OUT RHYME

Hinty, minty, cuty, corn,
Apple seed, and apple thorn,
Wire, briar, limber lock,
Three geese in a flock.
One flew east, and one flew west,
One flew over the cuckoo's nest.
  Up on yonder hill,
That is where my father dwells;
He has jewels, he has rings,
He has many pretty things.
He has a hammer with two nails,
He has a cat with twenty tails.
Strike Jack, lick Tom!
  Blow the bellows, old man!

— *Traditional: English*

75

A COUNTING-OUT RHYME

Silver bark of beech, and sallow
Bark of yellow birch and yellow
Twig of willow.

Stripe of green in moosewood maple,
Color seen in leaf of apple,
Bark of popple.

Wood of popple pale as moonbeam,
Wood of oak for yoke and barn beam,
Wood of hornbeam.

Silver bark of beech, and hollow
Stem of elder, tall and yellow
Twig of willow.

— *Edna St. Vincent Millay*

DRAW A PAIL OF WATER

Draw a pail of water
For my lady's daughter;
Her father's a king and her mother's a queen
Her two little sisters are dressed in green,
Stamping grass and parsley,
Marigold leaves and daisies.
One rush, two rush!
Pray thee, fine lady, come under my bush.

— *Traditional: English*

ROSY APPLE, LEMON OR PEAR

A SINGING-GAME RHYME

Rosy apple, lemon or pear,
Bunch of roses shall she wear;
Gold and silver by her side,
I know who will be the bride;
Take her by her lily-white hand,
Lead her to the altar;
Give her kisses, — one, two, three, —
Mother's runaway daughter.

— Traditional: English

RIDDLES

In marble halls as white as milk,
Lined with a skin as soft as silk,
Within a fountain crystal-clear,
A golden apple doth appear.
No doors there are to this stronghold,
Yet thieves break in and steal the gold.

— *Anonymous*

Answer: *An egg.*

Higgledy piggledy
Here we lie,
Pick'd and pluck'd,
And put in a pie.
My first is snapping, snarling, growling,
My second's industrious, romping, and prowling.
Higgledy piggledy
Here we lie,
Pick'd and pluck'd
And put in a pie.

Answer: *Currants (Cur. Rants).*

What shoemaker makes shoes without leather,
With all the four elements put together?
Fire and water, earth and air;
Ev'ry customer has two pair.

Answer: *A horse-shoer.*

— *Traditional: English*

Riddles from THE HOBBIT

What has roots as nobody sees,
Is taller than trees,
    Up, up it goes,
    And yet never grows?

('Easy!' said Bilbo. 'Mountain, I suppose.')

An eye in a blue face
Saw an eye in a green face.
'That eye is like to this eye'
Said the first eye,
'But in low place,
Not in high place.'

('Sun on the daisies it means, it does.')

It cannot be seen, cannot be felt,
Cannot be heard, cannot be smelt.
It lies behind stars and under hills,
    And empty holes it fills.
It comes first and follows after,
    Ends life, kills laughter.

('Dark!')

Alive without breath,
As cold as death;
Never thirsty, ever drinking,
All in mail never clinking.

('Ugh!' he said, 'it is cold and clammy!' — and so he
guessed. 'Fish! fish!' he cried. 'It is fish!')

This thing all things devours:
Birds, beasts, trees, flowers;
Gnaws iron, bites steel;
Grinds hard stones to meal;
Slays king, ruins town,
And beats high mountain down.

(. . . he wanted to shout out: 'Give me more time!
Give me time!' But all that came out with a sudden
squeal was:
                    'Time! Time!'
Bilbo was saved by pure luck. For that of course was
the answer.)

— *J. R. R. Tolkien*

LIMERICKS

An epicure, dining at Crewe,
Found quite a large mouse in his stew.
    Said the waiter, 'Don't shout
    And wave it about,
Or the rest will be wanting one too!'

        — Anonymous

There was an old lady of Steen,
Whose musical sense was not keen;
    She said, 'Well, it's odd,
    But I cannot tell "God
Save the Weasel" from "Pop Goes the Queen." '

        — Anonymous

There was a young woman named Bright,
Whose speed was much faster than light.
    She set out one day
    In a relative way,
And returned on the previous night.

        — Anonymous

There was an Old Man with a beard,
Who said, 'It is just as I feared! —
    Two Owls and a Hen,
    Four Larks and a Wren
Have all built their nests in my beard.'

        — Edward Lear

A tutor who tooted the flute
Tried to teach two young tooters to toot.
    Said the two to the tutor,
    'Is it harder to toot, or
To tutor two tooters to toot?'

        — Carolyn Wells

THE GNU

G. stands for Gnu, whose weapons of defence
Are long, sharp, curling horns, and common sense.
To these he adds a name so short and strong,
That even hardy Boers pronounce it wrong.
How often on a bright autumnal day
The pious people of Pretoria say
'Come, let us hunt the — ' then no more is heard,
But sounds of strong men struggling with a word;
Meanwhile the distant Gnu with grateful eyes
Observes his opportunity and flies.

— *Hilaire Belloc*

THE FROG

Be kind and tender to the Frog,
    And do not call him names,
As 'Slimy-skin,' or 'Polly-wog,'
    Or likewise 'Uncle James,'
Or 'Gape-a-grin,' or 'Toad-gone-wrong,'
    Or 'Billy-Bandy Knees':
The frog is justly sensitive
    To epithets like these.

No animal will more repay
    A treatment kind and fair,
At least so lonely people say
Who keep a frog (and by the way,
    They are extremely rare).

— *Hilaire Belloc*

from: 'SYLVIE AND BRUNO'

He thought he saw a Banker's clerk
    Descending from the 'bus;
He looked again, and found it was
    A Hippopotamus.
'If this should stay to dine,' he said,
    'There won't be much for us!'

He thought he saw an Albatross
    That fluttered round the lamp:
He looked again, and found it was
    A Penny-Postage-Stamp.
'You'd best be getting home,' he said;
    'The nights are very damp!'

He thought he saw a Coach-and-Four
    That stood beside his bed:
He looked again, and found it was
    A Bear without a Head.
'Poor thing,' he said, 'poor silly thing!
    It's waiting to be fed!'

He thought he saw a Kangaroo
    That worked a coffee-mill:
He looked again, and found it was
    A Vegetable-Pill.
'Were I to swallow this,' he said,
    'I should be very ill!'

He thought he saw a Rattlesnake
    That questioned him in Greek:
He looked again, and found it was
    The Middle of Next Week.
'The one thing I regret,' he said,
    'Is that it cannot speak!'

— Lewis Carroll

I SAW A PEACOCK

I saw a peacock with a fiery tail
I saw a blazing comet drop down hail
I saw a cloud wrappèd with ivy round
I saw an oak creep on along the ground
I saw a pismire swallow up a whale
I saw the sea brim full of ale
I saw a Venice glass full fathom deep
I saw a well full of men's tears that weep
I saw red eyes all of a flaming fire
I saw a house bigger than the moon and higher
I saw the sun at twelve o'clock at night
I saw the man that saw this wondrous sight.

— Unknown

Note: A little punctuation will reduce this pleasant fantasy to sober
common sense, not so much fun, but perhaps more satisfactory to some.

from: ALICE'S ADVENTURES IN WONDERLAND

'Stand up and repeat " *'Tis the voice of the sluggard,*" '[1]
said the Gryphon.

Alice got up, and began to repeat it, but her head was so
full of the Lobster-Quadrille that she hardly knew what she
was saying; and the words came very queer indeed: —

"'Tis the voice of the Lobster; I heard him declare
"You have baked me too brown, I must sugar my hair."
As a duck with his eyelids, so he with his nose
Trims his belt and his buttons, and turns out his toes;
When the sands are all dry, he is gay as a lark,
And will talk in contemptuous tones of the Shark:
But, when the tide rises and sharks are around,
His voice has a timid and tremulous sound.'

('That's different from what I used to say when I was
a child,' said the Gryphon.)

'I passed by his garden, and marked, with one eye,
How the Owl and the Panther were sharing a pie:
The Panther took pie-crust, and gravy and meat,
While the Owl had the dish as its share of the treat.
When the pie was all finished, the Owl, as a boon,
Was kindly permitted to pocket the spoon:
While the Panther received knife and fork with a growl,
And concluded the banquet by - - - - - - - - - - - '

('What *is* the use of repeating all that stuff?' the Mock
Turtle interrupted, 'if you don't explain it as you go on?
It's by far the most confusing thing I ever heard!')

— *Lewis Carroll*

[1] He meant 'The Sluggard,' by Isaac Watts.

85

THE SLUGGARD

'Tis the voice of a sluggard; I hear him complain —
'You have waked me too soon; I must slumber again';
As the door on its hinges, so he on his bed,
Turns his sides, and his shoulders, and his heavy head.
'A little more sleep, and a little more slumber' —
Thus he wastes half his days, and his hours without number;
And when he gets up, he sits folding his hands,
Or walks about saunt'ring, or trifling he stands.

I passed by his garden, and saw the wild brier
The thorn and the thistle grow broader and higher;
The clothes that hang on him are turning to rags;
And his money still wastes till he starves or he begs.

I made him a visit, still hoping to find
That he took better care for improving his mind;
He told me his dreams, talked of eating and drinking,
But he scarce reads his Bible, and never loves thinking.

Said I then to my heart: 'Here's a lesson for me;
That man's but a picture of what I might be;
But thanks to my friends for their care in my breeding,
Who taught me betimes to love working and reading.'

— Isaac Watts

♯ THREE LITTLE PIGS

Oh, the farmer had one,
And the farmer had two,
And the farmer had three
Little pigs in a stew,
　Tra-la-la.

They were wrapped up in batter,
They were wrapped up in dough,
They were stewed, they were spiced,
They were baked, O-ho!
　Tra-la-la.

When the piglets were finished,
The farmer looked in.
But he never could eat them
For fear 'twas a sin.
　Tra-la-la.

Oh, the pigs sang a carol,
The farmer joined in,
With the eating forgotten
Amidst all the din,
　Tra-la-la.

— Traditional: American

Collected by *John Jacob Niles*

OLD DUCKY QUACKEREL

Old Ducky Quackerel
Went to catch a mackerel;
    Toothsome fish,
    Dainty dish,
Make the wife a snackerel!

Old Ducky Quackerel
Took his fishing tackerel;
    Line and hook,
    Both he took,
Started down the trackerel.

Old Ducky Quackerel
Said, 'I have a knackerel!
    When I go
    Fishing so,
Food will never lackerel.'

Old Ducky Quackerel
Hooked a monstrous jackerel;
    Such a weight
    On the bait
Pulled him in ker-whackerel!

Old Ducky Quackerel
Let the line go slackerel.
    Flapped ashore,
    Never more
Will he go for mackerel!

— *Laura E. Richards*

♪ CALICO PIE

Calico Pie
The little Birds fly
Down to the calico tree,
 Their wings were blue,
 And they sang 'Tilly-loo!'
 Till away they flew, —
And they never came back to me!
 They never came back!
 They never came back!
They never came back to me!

Calico Jam
The little Fish swam
Over the syllabub sea,
 He took off his hat,
 To the Sole and the Sprat,
 And the Willeby-wat, —
But he never came back to me!
 He never came back!
 He never came back!
He never came back to me!

Calico Ban,
The little Mice ran,
To be ready in time for tea,
 Flippity flup,
 They drank it all up
 And danced in the cup, —
But they never came back to me!
 They never came back!
 They never came back!
They never came back to me!

Calico Drum,
The Grasshoppers come,
The Butterfly, Beetle, and Bee,
Over the ground,
Around and around,
With a hop and a bound, —
But they never came back!
They never came back!
They never came back!
They never came back to me!

— *Edward Lear*

LITTLE JOHN BOTTLEJOHN

Little John Bottlejohn lived on the hill,
   And a blithe little man was he.
And he won the heart of a pretty mermaid
   Who lived in the deep blue sea.
And every evening she used to sit
   And sing by the rocks of the sea,
'Oh! little John Bottlejohn, pretty John Bottlejohn,
   Won't you come out to me?'

Little John Bottlejohn heard her song,
   And he opened his little door.
And he hopped and he skipped, and he skipped and he
     hopped,
   Until he came down to the shore.
And there on the rocks sat the little mermaid,
   And still she was singing so free,
'Oh! little John Bottlejohn, pretty John Bottlejohn,
   Won't you come out to me?'

Little John Bottlejohn made a bow,
   And the mermaid, she made one too;
And she said, 'Oh! I never saw anyone half
   So perfectly sweet as you!
In my lovely home 'neath the ocean foam,
   How happy we both might be!
Oh! little John Bottlejohn, pretty John Bottlejohn,
   Won't you come down with me?'

Little John Bottlejohn said, 'Oh yes!
   I'll willingly go with you.
And I never shall quail at the sight of your tail,
   For perhaps I may grow one, too.'

So he took her hand, and he left the land,
    And plunged in the foaming main.
And little John Bottlejohn, pretty John Bottlejohn,
    Never was seen again.

— Laura E. Richards

from: THROUGH THE LOOKING-GLASS

'You are sad,' the Knight said in an anxious tone: 'let me sing you a song to comfort you.'

'Is it very long?' Alice asked, for she had heard a good deal of poetry that day.

'It's long,' said the Knight, 'but it's very, *very* beautiful. Everybody that hears me sing it — either it brings the *tears* into their eyes, or else — '

'Or else what?' said Alice, for the Knight had made a sudden pause.

'Or else it doesn't, you know. The name of the song is called *"Haddocks' Eyes."* '

'Oh, that's the name of the song, is it?' Alice said, trying to feel interested.

'No, you don't understand,' the Knight said, looking a little vexed. 'That's what the name is *called*. The name really *is "The Aged Aged Man."* '

'Then I ought to have said "That's what the *song* is called"?' Alice corrected herself.

'No, you oughtn't: that's quite another thing! The *song* is called *"Ways And Means"*: but that's only what it's *called,* you know!'

'Well, what *is* the song, then?' said Alice, who was by this time completely bewildered.

'I was coming to that,' the Knight said. 'The song really *is* "A-sitting On A Gate": and the tune's my own invention.'

. . . .

'But the tune *isn't* his own invention,' she said to herself: 'it's *"I give thee all, I can no more."* ' She stood and listened very attentively, but no tears came into her eyes.

    𝄞 'I'll tell thee everything I can:
       There's little to relate.
    I saw an aged aged man,
       A-sitting on a gate.
    "Who are you, aged man?" I said.
       "And how is it you live?"
    And his answer trickled through my head,
       Like water through a sieve.

    He said "I look for butterflies
       That sleep among the wheat:
    I make them into mutton-pies,
       And sell them in the street.
    I sell them unto men," he said,
       "Who sail on stormy seas;
    And that's the way I get my bread —
       A trifle, if you please."

    But I was thinking of a plan
       To dye one's whiskers green,
    And always use so large a fan
       That they could not be seen.
    So, having no reply to give
       To what the old man said,
    I cried "Come, tell me how you live!"
       And thumped him on the head.

His accents mild took up the tale:
  He said "I go my ways,
And when I find a mountain-rill,
  I set it in a blaze;
And thence they make a stuff they call
  Rowland's Macassar-Oil —
Yet twopence-halfpenny is all
  They give me for my toil."

But I was thinking of a way
  To feed oneself on batter,
And so go on from day to day
  Getting a little fatter.
I shook him well from side to side,
  Until his face was blue:
"Come, tell me how you live," I cried,
  "And what it is you do!"

He said 'I hunt for haddocks' eyes
  Among the heather bright,
And work them into waistcoat-buttons
  In the silent night.
And these I do not sell for gold
  Or coin of silvery shine,
But for a copper halfpenny,
  And that will purchase nine.

I sometimes dig for buttered rolls,
  Or set limed twigs for crabs:
I sometimes search the grassy knolls
  For wheels of Hansom-cabs.
And that's the way" (he gave a wink)
  "By which I get my wealth —
And very gladly will I drink
  Your Honour's noble health."

I heard him then, for I had just
    Completed my design
To keep the Menai bridge from rust
    By boiling it in wine.
I thanked him much for telling me
    The way he got his wealth,
But chiefly for his wish that he
    Might drink my noble health.

And now, if e'er by chance I put
    My fingers into glue,
Or madly squeeze a right-hand foot
    Into a left-hand shoe,
Or if I drop upon my toe
    A very heavy weight,
I weep for it reminds me so
Of that old man I used to know —
Whose look was mild, whose speech was **slow,**
Whose hair was whiter than the snow,
Whose face was very like a crow,
With eyes, like cinders, all aglow,
Who seemed distracted with his woe,
Who rocked his body to and fro,
And muttered mumblingly and low,
As if his mouth were full of dough,
Who snorted like a buffalo —
That summer evening long ago,
    A-sitting on a gate.'

                   — *Lewis Carroll*

THERE WAS A MAN OF NEWINGTON

There was a man of Newington,
  And he was wondrous wise,
He jumped into a gooseberry bush
  And scratched out both his eyes;
And when he saw his eyes were out,
  With all his might and main
He jumped into another bush
  And scratched them in again.

— *Unknown*

THERE WAS A MAN AND HE HAD NOUGHT

There was a man and he had nought,
And robbers came to rob him;
He crept up to the chimney-pot,
And then they thought they had him.

But he got down on t'other side,
And then they could not find him.
He ran fourteen miles in fifteen days,
And never looked behind him.

— *Traditional: English*

THE BLIND MEN AND THE ELEPHANT

(A HINDOO FABLE)

It was six men of Indostan
  To learning much inclined,
Who went to see the Elephant
  (Though all of them were blind),
That each by observation
  Might satisfy his mind.

The *First* approached the Elephant,
  And happening to fall
Against his broad and sturdy side,
  At once began to bawl:
'God bless me! but the Elephant
  Is very like a wall!'

The *Second*, feeling at the tusk,
  Cried, 'Ho! what have we here
So very round and smooth and sharp?
  To me 'tis mighty clear
This wonder of an Elephant
  Is very like a spear!'

The *Third* approached the animal,
  And happening to take
The squirming trunk within his hands,
  Thus boldly up and spake:
'I see,' quoth he, 'the Elephant
  Is very like a snake!'

The *Fourth* reached out an eager hand,
  And felt about the knee.

'What most this wondrous beast is like
  Is mighty plain,' quoth he;
''Tis clear enough the Elephant
  Is very like a tree!'

The *Fifth* who chanced to touch the ear,
  Said: 'E'en the blindest man
Can tell what this resembles most;
  Deny the fact who can,
This marvel of an Elephant
  Is very like a fan!'

The *Sixth* no sooner had begun
  About the beast to grope,
Than, seizing on the swinging tail
  That fell within his scope,
'I see,' quoth he, 'The Elephant
  Is very like a rope!'

And so these men of Indostan
  Disputed loud and long,
Each in his own opinion
  Exceeding stiff and strong,
Though each was partly in the right,
  And all were in the wrong!

Moral

So oft in theologic wars,
  The disputants, I ween,
Rail on in utter ignorance
  Of what the others mean,
*And prate about an Elephant
  Not one of them has seen!*

— *John Godfrey Saxe*

THE OLD TAILOR

There was once an old Tailor of Hickery Mo,
Too tired at evening to sew, to sew;
He put by his needle, he snapped his thread,
And, cross-legged, sang to his fiddle instead.
His candle bobbed at each note that came
And spat out a spark from the midst of its flame;
His catgut strings they yelped and yawled,
The wilder their scrapings the louder he bawled;
The grease trickled over at every beat,
Welled down to the stick in a winding-sheet —
Till up sprang Puss from the fire, with a WOW!
'A *fine* kakkamangul you're making now!'

— *Walter de la Mare*

THE PRINCE

Sweet Peridarchus was a Prince,
The Prince he was of — Mouses;
He roved and roamed the haunts of **Men,**
And ranged about their houses.

He gnawed his way along a street,
Through holes in every wainscot,
Fandangoed in the attics and
From basement on to basement.

His eyes like bits of rubies shone;
His coat, as sleek as satin —
With teeth as sharp as needle-points —
He kept to keep him fat in.

His squeak so sharp in the small hours **rang**
That every waker wondered;
He trimmed his whiskers stiff as wire,
Had sweethearts by the hundred.

He'd gut a Cheshire cheese with ease,
Plum cake devoured in slices,
Lard, haggis, suet, sausages,
And everything that nice is.

Cork out, he'd dangle down his tail
For oil that was in bottle;
Nothing too sweet, nothing too fat
For Peridarchus' throttle.

He'd dance upon a chimney-pot,
The merry stars a-twinkling;

Or, scampering up a chandelier,
Set all the lustres tinkling.

He'd skip into a pianoforte
To listen how it sounded;
He bored into a butt of wine,
And so was nearly drownded.

At midnight when he sat at meat,
Twelve saucy, sonsy maidens,
With bee-sweet voices, ditties sang,
Some sad ones, and some gay ones.

For bodyguard he had a score
Of warriors grim and hardy;
They raided every larder round,
From Peebles to — Cromàrty.

Grimalkin — deep in dreams she lay,
Comes he, with these gay friskers,
Steals up and gnaws away her claws,
And plucks out all her whiskers.

He scaled a bell-rope where there snored
The Bailiff and his Lady;
Danced on his nose, nibbled her toes,
And kissed the squalling Baby.

A merry life was his, I trow,
Despite it was a short one;
One night he met a mort of rats —
He bared his teeth, and fought one:

A bully ruffian, thrice his size;
But when the conflict ended,
He sighed, 'Alack, my back is broke,
And that can ne'er be mended.'

They laid him lifeless on a bier,
They lapped him up in ermine;
They lit a candle, inches thick,
His Uncle preached the sermon.

'O Mouseland, mourn for him that's gone,
Our noble Peridarchus!
In valiant fight but yesternight,
And now, alas, a carcass!

'A Hero, Mouse or Man, is one
Who never wails or winces;
Friends, shed a tear for him that's here,
The Princeliest of Princes!'

— Walter de la Mare

THE STORY OF THE GRAY GOOSE

A fox went out in a hungry plight,
And he begged of the moon to give him light,
For he'd many miles to trot that night
    Before he could reach his den, O!

And first he came to a farmer's yard,
Where the ducks and geese declared it hard
That their nerves should be shaken and their rest be marred
    By the visit of Mister Fox, O!

He took the gray goose by the sleeve;
Says he, 'Madam Goose, and by your leave,
I'll take you away without reprieve,
    And carry you home to my den, O!'

He seized the black duck by the neck,
And swung her all across his back;
The black duck cried out, 'Quack! quack! quack!'
    With her legs hanging dangling down, O!

Then old Mrs. Slipper-slopper jumped out of bed,
And out of the window she popped her head, —
'John, John, John, the gray goose is gone,
    And the fox is off to his den, O!'

Then John he went up to the hill,
And he blew a blast both loud and shrill.
Says the fox, 'This is very pretty music — still
    I'd rather be at my den, O!'

At last the fox got home to his den;
To his dear little foxes, eight, nine, ten,

Says he, 'You're in luck; here's a good fat duck,
  With her legs hanging dangling down, O!'

He then sat down with his hungry wife;
They did very well without fork or knife;
They never ate a better goose in all their life,
  And the little ones picked the bones, O!

— Traditional: English

♪ THE DERBY RAM

As I was going to Derby, Sir, 'twas on a summer's day,
I met the finest ram, Sir, that ever was fed on hay;
  And indeed, Sir, 'tis true, Sir, I never was given to lie,
  And if you'd been to Derby, Sir, you'd have seen him as
    well as I.

It had four feet to walk on, Sir, it had four feet to stand,
And every foot it had, Sir, did cover an acre of land.
  And indeed, Sir, 'tis true, Sir, I never was given to lie,
  And if you'd been to Derby, Sir, you'd have seen him as
    well as I.

The horns that were on its head, Sir, held a regiment of
    men,
And the tongue that was in its head, Sir, would feed them
    every one.
  And indeed, Sir, 'tis true, Sir, I never was given to lie,
  And if you'd been to Derby, Sir, you'd have seen him as
    well as I.

The wool that was on its back, Sir, made fifty packs of cloth,
And for to tell a lie, Sir, I'm sure I'm very loth.

And indeed, Sir, 'tis true, Sir, for I never was given to lie,
And if you'd been to Derby, Sir, you'd have seen him as
   well as I.

The wool that was on its sides, Sir, made fifty more
   complete,
And it was sent to Russia to clothe the Emperor's fleet.
   And indeed, Sir, 'tis true, Sir, for I never was given to lie,
   And if you'd been to Derby, Sir, you'd have seen him as
      well as I.

The tail was fifty yards, Sir, as near as I can tell,
And it was sent to Rome, Sir, to ring Saint Peter's bell.
   And indeed, Sir, 'tis true, Sir, for I never was given to lie,
   And if you'd been to Derby, Sir, you'd have seen him as
      well as I.

— Traditional: English

THE RIDDLING KNIGHT

There were three sisters fair and bright,
Jennifer, Gentle and Rosemary,
And they three loved one valiant knight —
As the dew flies over the mulberry-tree.

The eldest sister let him in,
Jennifer, Gentle and Rosemary,
And barr'd the door with a silver pin,
As the dew flies over the mulberry-tree.

The second sister made his bed,
Jennifer, Gentle and Rosemary,
And placed soft pillows under his head,
As the dew flies over the mulberry-tree.

The youngest sister that same night,
Jennifer, Gentle and Rosemary,
Was resolved for to wed wi' this valiant **knight,**
As the dew flies over the mulberry-tree.

'And if you can answer questions three,
Jennifer, Gentle and Rosemary,
O then, fair maid, I'll marry wi' thee,
As the dew flies over the mulberry-tree.

'O what is louder nor a horn,
Jennifer, Gentle and Rosemary,
O what is sharper nor a thorn?
As the dew flies over the mulberry-tree.

'Or what is heavier nor the lead,
Jennifer, Gentle and Rosemary,

Or what is better nor the bread?
As the dew flies over the mulberry-tree.

'Or what is longer nor the way,
Jennifer, Gentle and Rosemary,
Or what is deeper nor the sea?' —
As the dew flies over the mulberry-tree.

'O shame is louder nor a horn,
Jennifer, Gentle and Rosemary,
And hunger is sharper nor a thorn,
As the dew flies over the mulberry-tree.

'O sin is heavier nor the lead,
Jennifer, Gentle and Rosemary,
The blessing's better nor the bread,
As the dew flies over the mulberry-tree.

'O the wind is longer nor the way,
Jennifer, Gentle and Rosemary,
And love is deeper nor the sea,'
As the dew flies over the mulberry-tree.

'You have answer'd my questions three.
Jennifer, Gentle and Rosemary;
And now, fair maid, I'll marry wi' thee,'
As the dew flies over the mulberry-tree.

— Traditional: English

𝄞 RIDDLES WISELY EXPOUNDED
OR
THE DEVIL'S TEN QUESTIONS

If you don't answer my questions well,
  Sing ninety-nine and ninety,
I'll take you off, and I live in Hell,
  And you the weavering bonty.

Oh, what is whiter far than milk?
  Sing ninety-nine and ninety!
And what is softer far than silk?
  And you the weavering bonty!

Oh, snow is whiter far than milk,
  Sing ninety-nine and ninety!
And down is softer far than silk,
  And me the weavering bonty!

Oh, what is louder than a horn?
  Sing ninety-nine and ninety!
And what is sharper than a thorn?
  And you the weavering bonty!

Oh, thunder's louder than a horn,
  Sing ninety-nine and ninety,
And death is sharper than a thorn,
  And me the weavering bonty!

Oh, what is higher than a tree?
  Sing ninety-nine and ninety!
And what is deeper than the sea?
  And you the weavering bonty!

110

Oh, Heaven's higher than a tree,
   Sing ninety-nine and ninety,
And Hell is deeper than the sea,
   And me the weavering bonty.

Oh, what red fruit September grows?
   Sing ninety-nine and ninety!
And what thing round the whole world goes?
   And you the weavering bonty!

The apple in September grows,
   Sing ninety-nine and ninety,
And the air around the whole world goes,
   And me the weavering bonty.

Oh, what is wicked man's repay?
   Sing ninety-nine and ninety!
And what is worse than woman's way?
   And you the weavering bonty.

Now Hell is wicked man's repay,
   Sing ninety-nine and ninety,
And a she-devil's worse than woman's way,
   And me the weavering bonty.

Oh, you have answered my question well,
   Sing ninety-nine and ninety!
But I'll take you off, 'cause I live in Hell,
   And you the weavering bonty.

                — Traditional: American

Collected by *John Jacob Niles*

𝄞 GREEN GROW THE RUSHES, OH!

First Voice: I'll sing you one, oh!
                      Green grow the rushes, oh!

Second Voice: What is your one, oh?

First Voice: One is one and all alone,
                      And evermore shall be so.

First Voice: I'll sing you two, oh!
                      Green grow the rushes, oh!

Second Voice: What is your two, oh?

First Voice: Two, two, the lily-white boys,
                      Clothed all in green, oh!
                      One is one and all alone,
                      And evermore shall be so.

First Voice: I'll sing you three, oh!
                      Green grow the rushes, oh!

Second Voice: What is your three, oh?

First Voice: Three, three, the rivals,
                      Two, two the lily-white boys,
                      Clothed all in green, oh!
                      One is one and all alone,
                      And evermore shall be so.

First Voice: I'll sing you four, oh!
                      Green grow the rushes, oh!

Second Voice: What is your four, oh?

First Voice: Four for the Gospel Makers,
                      Three, three, the rivals,
                      Two, two, the lily-white boys

Clothed all in green, oh!
One is one and all alone,
And evermore shall be so.

First Voice: I'll sing you five, oh!
Green grow the rushes, oh!

Second Voice: What is your five, oh?

First Voice: Five for the symbols at your door
And four for the Gospel Makers,
Three, three, the rivals,
Two, two, the lily-white boys
Clothed all in green, oh!
One is one and all alone,
And evermore shall be so.

First Voice: I'll sing you six, oh!
Green grow the rushes, oh!

Second Voice: What is your six, oh?

First Voice: Six for the six proud walkers,
Five for the symbols at your door
And four for the Gospel Makers,
Three, three, the rivals,
Two, two, the lily-white boys
Clothed all in green, oh!
One is one and all alone
And evermore shall be so.

First Voice: I'll sing you seven, oh!
Green grow the rushes, oh!

Second Voice: What is your seven, oh?

First Voice: Seven for the seven stars in the sky,
And six for the six proud walkers,

Five for the symbols at your door
And four for the Gospel Makers,
Three, three, the rivals,
Two, two, the lily-white boys
Clothed all in green, oh!
One is one and all alone
And evermore shall be so.

First Voice: I'll sing you eight, oh!
Green grow the rushes, oh!

Second Voice: What is your eight, oh?

First Voice: Eight for the April rainers,
Seven for the seven stars in the sky,
And six for the six proud walkers,
Five for the symbols at your door,
And four for the Gospel Makers,
Three, three, the rivals,
Two, two, the lily-white boys
Clothed all in green, oh!
One is one and all alone
And evermore shall be so.

First Voice: I'll sing you nine, oh!
Green grow the rushes, oh!

Second Voice: What is your nine, oh?

First Voice: Nine for the nine that brightly shine,
And eight for the April rainers,
Seven for the seven stars in the sky,
And six for the six proud walkers,
Five for the symbols at your door,
And four for the Gospel Makers,
Three, three, the rivals,
Two, two, the lily-white boys

114

Clothed all in green, oh!
One is one and all alone
And evermore shall be so.

First Voice: I'll sing you ten, oh!
Green grow the rushes, oh!

Second Voice: What is your ten, oh?

First Voice: Ten for the Ten Commandments,
Nine for the nine that brightly shine
And eight for the April rainers,
Seven for the seven stars in the sky,
And six for the six proud walkers,
Five for the symbols at your door,
And four for the Gospel Makers,
Three, three, the rivals,
Two, two, the lily-white boys
Clothed all in green, oh!
One is one and all alone
And evermore shall be so.

First Voice: I'll sing you twelve, oh!
Green grow the rushes, oh!

Second Voice: What is your twelve, oh?

First Voice: Twelve for the twelve Apostles,
Eleven for the eleven that went to heaven
And ten for the Ten Commandments,
Nine for the nine that brightly shine
And eight for the April rainers,
Seven for the seven stars in the sky,
And six for the six proud walkers,
Five for the symbols at your door,
And four for the Gospel Makers,
Three, three, the rivals,

Two, two, the lily-white boys
Clothed all in green, oh!
One is one and all alone
And evermore shall be so.

— Traditional: English

Note on 'Green Grow the Rushes, Oh!'

These are the words of a song with a very long history, which so far as
we know has not yet been completely traced. It is found in a great variety
of different and curious forms in very many languages both ancient and
modern, from Hebrew on down. The meanings given here are those
sifted out by authorities on such things, but it must be remembered that
any song as old as this one strays from original words and meanings
through being sung so often from hearsay and memory. Sometimes ver-
sions are heard quite different from those given here.

1. Essentially the same in all versions — God Almighty.
2. The Hebrew version gives 'Two for the Tables of the Law.' The
   version given here is considered to be an allusion to Christ and
   John the Baptist.
3. Sometimes heard as 'Three, three the Wisers,' meaning the Wise
   Men. The version given is commonly accepted as meaning the
   Persons of the Trinity: Father, Son and Holy Spirit.
4. The Gospel Makers, Matthew, Mark, Luke and John.
5. The Pentacle (or Pentagram), a five-pointed star supposed to have
   mystical properties, and often inscribed on thresholds in former
   times to keep away the Evil One.
6. A corruption of 'waters' or 'water-pots' (sometimes given as 'bold,'
   'cheerful,' or 'charming'). The reference is to the six water-pots
   used in the miracle of changing water into wine at Cana of
   Galilee.
7. The seven stars that form the constellation of The Great Bear.
8. Sometimes given as 'eight bold rainers' or 'rangers'; 'bright shiners';
   'archangels'; 'angel-givers,' or 'Gabriel angels.' Probably has ref-
   erence to angels, although the significance of the number is not
   clear.
9. Some versions give 'tentmakers,' 'Kings of Lunnery' or 'maiden
   muses' — of which only the 'maiden muses' (the Nine Muses) has
   any traceable meaning. The version given here has no apparent
   meaning, but makes a pleasant sound.

116

10. No version other than this is known.
11. This number is left out when 'singing up,' as an expression of contempt for Judas Iscariot, who presumably did not go to heaven.
12. The only known version except for the Hebrew, which gives the Twelve Tribes of Israel.

𝄞 THE FOUR PRESENTS

I had four brothers over the sea,
Perrie, Merrie, Dixi, Domine;
And they each sent a present unto me.
Petrum, Partrum, Paradisi Tempore,
Perrie, Merrie, Dixi, Domine.

The first sent a goose without a bone,
Perrie, Merrie, Dixi, Domine,
The second sent a cherry without a stone,
Petrum, Partrum, Paradisi Tempore,
Perrie, Merrie, Dixi, Domine.

The third sent a blanket without a thread,
Perrie, Merrie, Dixi, Domine,
The fourth sent a book no man could read,
Petrum, Partrum, Paradisi Tempore,
Perrie, Merrie, Dixi, Domine.

When the cherry's in the blossom there is no stone,
Perrie, Merrie, Dixi, Domine,
When the goose is in the egg-shell, there is no bone,
Petrum, Partrum, Paradisi Tempore,
Perrie, Merrie, Dixi, Domine.

When the wool's on the sheep's back there's no thread,
  Perrie, Merrie, Dixi, Domine,
When the book's in the press, no man it can read,
  Petrum, Partrum, Paradisi Tempore,
  Perrie, Merrie, Dixi, Domine.

— *Traditional: English*

HYND ETIN

May Margaret sits in her bower door,
  Sewing her silken seam;
She heard a note in Elmond's wood,
  And wish'd she there had been.

She loot the seam fa' frae her side,
  The needle to her tae,
And she is on to Elmond's wood
  As fast as she could gae.

She hadna pu'd a nut, a nut,
  Nor broken a branch but ane,
Till by there came the Hynd Etin,
  Says, 'Lady, lat alane.

'O why pu' ye the nut, the nut,
  Or why brake ye the tree?
For I am forester o' this wood:
  Ye should spier leave at me.'

'I'll ask leave at nae living man,
  Nor yet will I at thee;
My father is king o'er a' this realm,
  This wood belongs to me.'

loot: let   *tae*: toe   *lat*: let   *spier*: ask

118

The highest tree in Elmond's wood,
   He's pu'd it by the reet,
And he has built for her a bower
   Near by a hallow seat.

He's kept her there in Elmond's wood,
   For six lang years and ane,
Till six pretty sons to him she bare,
   And the seventh she's brought hame.

It fell out ance upon a day
   He's to the hunting gane,
And a' to carry his game for him
   He's tane his eldest son.

'A question I would ask, father,
   Gin ye wadna angry be.' —
'Say on, say on, my bonny boy,
   Ye'se nae be quarrell'd by me.'

'I see my mither's cheeks aye weet,
   I never see them dry;
And I wonder what aileth my mither
   To mourn sae constantly.' —

'Your mither was a king's daughtèr,
   Sprung frae a high degree;
She might hae wed some worthy prince
   Had she nae been stown by me.

'Your mither was a king's daughtèr
   Of noble birth and fame,
But now she's wife of Hynd Etin,
   Wha ne'er got christendame.

reet: root   *gin*: if   *stown*: stolen

'But we'll shoot the buntin' o' the bush,
  The linnet o' the tree,
And ye'se tak' them hame to your dear mither
  See if she'll merrier be.'

It fell upon anither day,
  He's to the hunting gane
And left his seven young children
  To stay with their mither at hame.

'O I will tell you, mither,
  Gin ye wadna angry be.' —
'Speak on, speak on, my little wee boy,
  Ye'se nae be quarrell'd by me.' —

'As we came frae the hind-hunting,
  We heard fine music ring.' —
'My blessings on you, my bonny boy,
  I wish I'd been there my lane.'

They wistna weel where they were gaen,
  Wi' the stratlins o' their feet;
They wistna weel where they were gaen,
  Till at her father's yate.

'I hae nae miney in my pocket,
  But royal rings hae three;
I'll gie them you, my little young son,
  And ye'll walk there for me.

'Ye'll gie the first to the proud portèr
  And he will let you in;

lane: lone (*him lane*, by himself)   *wist, wistna*: knew, knew not
yate: gate

120

Ye'll gie the next to the butler-boy
    And he will show you ben.

'Ye'll gie the third to the minstrel
    That plays before the King;
He'll play success to the bonny boy
    Came thro' the wood him lane.'

He ga'e the first to the proud portèr
    And he open'd and let him in;
He ga'e the next to the butler-boy,
    And he has shown him ben.

He ga'e the third to the minstrel
    That played before the King,
And he play'd success to the bonny boy
    Came thro' the wood him lane.

Now when he came before the King,
    Fell low upon his knee;
The King he turn'd him round about,
    And the saut tear blint his e'e.

'Win up, win up, my bonny boy,
    Gang frae my companie;
Ye look sae like my dear daughtèr,
    My heart will burst in three.' —

'If I look like your dear daughtèr,
    A wonder it is none;
If I look like your dear daughtèr,
    I am her eldest son.'

ben: (into) the inner room
win up: get up

'Will ye tell me, ye little wee boy,
  Where may my Margaret be?' —
'She's just now standing at your yates,
  And my six brithers her wi'.' —

'O where are a' my porter-boys
  That I pay meat and fee,
To open my yates baith wide and braid,
  Let her come in to me?'

When she cam' in before the King,
  Fell low down on her knee:
'Win up, win up, my daughter dear,
  This day ye'se dine wi' me.'

'Ae bit I canna eat, father,
  Nor ae drop can I drink,
Until I see my mither dear,
  For lang for her I think.'

When she cam' in before the queen,
  Fell low down on her knee;
'Win up, win up, my daughter dear,
  This day ye'se dine wi' me.' —

'Ae bit I canna eat, mither,
  Nor ae drop can I drink,
Until I see my sister dear,
  For lang for her I think.'

When that these twa sisters met,
  She hailed her courteouslie;
'Come be, come be, my sister dear,
  This day ye'se dine wi' me.' —

ye'se: you shall (singular)

'Ae bit I canna eat, sister,
  Nor ae drop can I drink,
Until I see my dear husband,
  So lang for him I think.' —

'O where are a' my rangers bold
  That I pay meat and fee,
To search the forest far an' wide,
  And bring back Etin to me?'

Out it speaks the little wee boy:
  'Na, na, this mauna be;
Without ye grant a free pardon,
  I hope ye'll nae him see.' —

'O here I grant a free pardon,
  Well seal'd by my own han';
Ye may mak' a search for Young Etin
  As soon as ever ye can.'

They search'd the country wide and braid,
  The forests far and near,
And they found him into Elmond's wood,
  Tearing his yellow hair.

'Win up, win up now, Hynd Etin,
  Win up an' boun wi' me;
We're messengers come frae the court;
  The King wants you to see.' —

'O let them tak' frae me my head,
  Or hang me on a tree;
For since I've lost my dear lady,
  Life's no pleasure to me.' —

boun: go

123

'Your head will na be touch'd, **Etin**,
    Nor you hang'd on a tree;
Your lady's in her father's court
    And a' he wants is thee.'

When he cam' in before the King,
    Fell low down on his knee;
'Win up, win up now, Young **Etin**,
    This day ye'se dine wi' me.'

But as they were at dinner set
    The wee boy ask'd a boon:
'I wish we were in a good kirk
    For to get christendoun.

'For we hae lived in gude green wood
    This seven years and ane;
But a' this time since e'er I mind
    Was never a kirk within.' —

'Your asking's nae sae great, my boy,
    But granted it sall be;
This day to gude kirk ye sall gang
    And your mither sall gang you wi'.'

When unto the gude kirk she came,
    She at the door did stan';
She was sae sair sunk down wi' shame,
    She couldna come farther ben.

Then out and spak' the parish priest,
    And a sweet smile ga'e he:
'Come ben, come ben, my lily-flower,
    Present your babes to me.'

Charles, Vincent, Sam and Dick,
  And likewise John and James;
They call'd the eldest Young Etin,
  Which was his father's name.

— *Traditional: Scots*

MOY CASTLE

There are seven men in Moy Castle
  Are merry men this night;
There are seven men in Moy Castle
  Whose hearts are gay and light.

Prince Charlie came to Moy Castle
  And asked for shelter there,
And down came Lady M'Intosh,
  As proud as she was fair.

'I'm a hunted man, Lady M'Intosh —
  A price is on my head!
If Lord Loudon knew thou'dst sheltered me,
  Both thou and I were sped.'

'Come in! come in, my prince!' said she,
  And opened wide the gate;
'To die with Prince Charlie Stuart,
  I ask no better fate.'

She's called her seven trusty men,
  The blacksmith at their head:
'Ye shall keep watch in the castle wood,
  To save our prince from dread.'

The lady has led the prince away,
    To make him royal cheer;
The seven men of M'Intosh
    Have sought the forest drear.

And there they looked and listened,
    Listened and looked amain;
And they heard the sound of the falling leaves,
    And the soft sound of the rain.

The blacksmith knelt beside an oak,
    And laid his ear to the ground,
And under the noises of the wood
    He heard a distant sound.

He heard the sound of many feet,
    Warily treading the heather —
He heard the sound of many men
    Marching softly together.

'There's no time now to warn the prince,
    The castle guards are few;
'Tis wit will win the play tonight,
    And what we here can do.'

He's gi'en the word to his six brethren,
    And through the wood they're gone;
The seven men of M'Intosh
    Each stood by himself alone.

'And he who has the pipes at his back,
    His best now let him play;
And he who has no pipes at his back,
    His best word let him say.'

It was five hundred Englishmen
   Were treading the purple heather,
Five hundred of Lord Loudon's men
   Marching softly together.

'There's none tonight in Moy Castle
   But servants poor and old;
If we bring the prince to Loudon's lord,
   He'll fill our hands with gold.'

They came lightly on their way,
   Had never a thought of ill,
When suddenly from the darksome wood
   Broke out a whistle shrill.

And straight the wood was filled with cries,
   With shouts of angry men,
And the angry skirl of the bagpipes
   Came answering the shouts again.

The Englishmen looked and listened,
   Listened and looked amain,
And nought could they see through the mirk night,
   But the pipes shrieked out again.

'Hark to the slogan of Lochiel,
   To Keppoch's gathering cry!
Hark to the rising swell that tells
   Clanranald's men are nigh!

'Now woe to the men that told us
   Lochiel was far away!
The whole of the Highland army
   Is waiting to bar our way.

127

'It's little we'll see of Charlie Stuart,
    And little of Loudon's gold,
And but we're away from this armed wood,
    Our lives have but little hold.'

It was five hundred Englishmen,
    They turned their faces and ran,
And well for him with the swiftest foot,
    For he was the lucky man.

And woe to him that was lame or slow,
    For they trampled him on the heather!
And back to the place from whence they came
    They're hirpling all together.

Lord Loudon's men, they are gone full far,
    Over the brow of the hill;
The seven men of M'Intosh,
    Their pipes are crying still.

They leaned them to a tree and laughed,
    'Twould do you good to hear,
And they are away to Moy Castle
    To tell their lady dear.

And who but Lady M'Intosh
    Would praise her men so bold?
And who but Prince Charlie Stuart
    Would count the good French gold?

There are seven men in Moy Castle
    Are joyful men this night;
There are seven men in Moy Castle
    Whose hearts will aye be light.

— *Traditional: Scots*

THE WAR SONG OF DINAS VAWR

The mountain sheep are sweeter,
But the valley sheep are fatter;
We therefore deemed it meeter
To carry off the latter.
We made an expedition;
We met a host and quelled it;
We forced a strong position,
And killed the men who held it.

On Dyfed's richest valley,
Where herds of kine were browsing,
We made a mighty sally,
To furnish our carousing.
Fierce warriors rushed to meet us;
We met them, and o'erthrew them:
They struggled hard to beat us;
But we conquered them, and slew them.

As we drove our prize at leisure,
The king marched forth to catch us:
His rage surpassed all measure,
But his people could not match us.
He fled to his hall-pillars;
And, ere our force we led off,
Some sacked his house and cellars,
While others cut his head off.

We there, in strife bewildering,
Spilt blood enough to swim in:
We orphaned many children,
And widowed many women.

The eagles and the ravens
We glutted with our foemen:
The heroes and the cravens,
The spearmen and the bowmen.

We brought away from battle,
And much their land bemoaned them,
Two thousand head of cattle,
And the head of him who owned them:
Edynfed, King of Dyfed,
His head was borne before us;
His wine and beasts supplied our feasts,
And his overthrow, our chorus.

— *Thomas Love Peacock*

from: *The Misfortunes of Elphin*

130

ROBIN HOOD RESCUING THE WIDOW'S THREE SONS

There are twelve months in all the year,
    As I hear many say,
But the merriest month in all the year
    Is the merry month of May.

Now Robin Hood is to Nottingham gone,
    With a link and a down, and a day,
And there he met a silly old woman,
    Was weeping on the way.

'What news? what news? thou silly old woman,
    What news hast thou for me?'
Said she, 'There's my three sons in Nottingham town
    Today condemned to die.'

'O, have they parishes burnt?' he said,
    'Or have they ministers slain?
Or have they robbèd any virgin?
    Or other men's wives have ta'en'?

'They have no parishes burnt, good sir,
    Nor yet have ministers slain,
Nor have they robbèd any virgin,
    Nor other men's wives have ta'en.'

'O, what have they done?' said Robin Hood,
    'I pray thee tell to me.'
'It's for slaying of the king's fallow deer,
    Bearing their long bows with thee.'

silly: simple.

'Dost thou not mind, old woman,' he said,
    'How thou madest me sup and dine?
By the truth of my body,' quoth Robin Hood,
    'You could not tell it in better time.'

Now Robin Hood is to Nottingham gone,
    With a link and a down, and a day,
And there he met with a silly old palmer,
    Was walking along the highway.

'What news? what news? thou silly old man,
    What news, I do thee pray?'
Said he, 'Three squires in Nottingham town
    Are condemned to die this day.'

'Come change thy apparel with me, old man,
    Come change thy apparel for mine;
Here is ten shillings in good silver,
    Go drink it in beer or wine.'

'O, thine apparel is good,' he said,
    'And mine is ragged and torn;
Wherever you go, wherever you ride,
    Laugh not an old man to scorn.'

'Come change thy apparel with me, old churl,
    Come change thy apparel with mine;
Here is a piece of good broad gold,
    Go feast thy brethren with wine.'

Then he put on the old man's hat,
    It stood full high in the crown:
'The first good bargain that I come at,
    It shall make thee come down.'

Then he put on the old man's cloak,
　　Was patch'd black, blue and red;
He thought it no shame all the day long,
　　To wear the bags of bread.

Then he put on the old man's breeks,
　　Was patch'd from leg to side;
'By the truth of my body,' bold Robin gan say,
　　'This man loved little pride.'

Then he put on the old man's hose,
　　Were patched from knee to wrist;
'By the truth of my body,' said bold Robin Hood,
　　'I'd laugh if I had any list.'

Then he put on the old man's shoes,
　　Were patch'd both beneath and aboon;
Then Robin Hood swore a solemn oath,
　　'It's good habit that makes a man.'

Now Robin Hood is to Nottingham gone,
　　With a link a down, and a down,
And there he met with the proud sheriff,
　　Was walking along the town.

'Save you, save you, sheriff!' he said
　　'Now heaven you save and see!
And what will you give to a silly old man
　　Today will your hangman be?'

'Some suits, some suits,' the sheriff he said,
　　'Some suits I'll give to thee;
Some suits, some suits, and pence thirteen,
　　Today's a hangman's fee.'

Then Robin he turns him round about,
     And jumps from stock to stone;
'By the truth of my body,' the sheriff he said,
     'That's well jumpt, thou nimble old man.'

'I was ne'er a hangman in all my life,
     Nor yet intends to trade;
But curst be he,' said bold Robin,
     'That first a hangman was made.'

'I've a bag for meal, and a bag for malt,
     And a bag for barley and corn;
A bag for bread, and a bag for beef,
     And a bag for my little small horn.'

'I have a horn in my pocket,
     I got it from Robin Hood,
And still when I set it to my mouth,
     For thee it blows little good.'

'O, wind thy horn, thou proud fellow!
     Of thee I have no doubt.
I wish that thou give such a blast,
     Till both thy eyes fall out.'

The first loud blast that he did blow,
     He blew both loud and shrill;
A hundred and fifty of Robin Hood's men
     Came riding over the hill.

The next loud blast that he did give,
     He blew both loud and amain,
And quickly sixty of Robin Hood's men
     Came shining over the plain.

'O, who are those,' the sheriff he said,
    'Come tripping over the lee?'
'They're my attendants,' brave Robin did say;
    'They'll pay a visit to thee.'

They took the gallows from the slack,
    They set it in the glen,
They hangèd the proud sheriff on that,
    Released their own three men.

— *Traditional: English*

♪ A SONG OF SHERWOOD

Sherwood in the twilight, is Robin Hood awake?
Grey and ghostly shadows are gliding through the brake,
Shadows of the dappled deer, dreaming through the morn,
Dreaming of a shadowy man that winds a shadowy horn.

Robin Hood is here again; all his merry thieves
Hear a ghostly bugle-note shivering through the leaves,
Calling as he used to call, faint and far away,
In Sherwood, in Sherwood, about the break of day.

Merry, merry England has kissed the lips of June;
All the wings of fairyland were here beneath the moon,
Like a flight of rose-leaves fluttering in a mist
Of opal and ruby and pearl and amethyst.

Merry, merry England is waking as of old,
With eyes of blither hazel and hair of brighter gold;
For Robin Hood is here again beneath the bursting spray
In Sherwood, in Sherwood, about the break of day.

Love is in the greenwood building him a house
Of wild rose and hawthorn and honeysuckle boughs;
Love is in the greenwood, dawn is in the skies,
And Marian is waiting with a glory in her eyes.

Hark! The dazzled laverock climbs the golden steep!
Marian is waiting; is Robin Hood asleep?
Round the fairy grass-rings frolic elf and fay,
In Sherwood, in Sherwood, about the break of day.

Oberon, Oberon, rake away the gold,
Rake away the red leaves, roll away the mould,
Rake away the gold leaves, roll away the red,
And wake Will Scarlett from his leafy forest bed.

Friar Tuck and Little John are riding down together
With quarter-staff and drinking-can and grey goose feather.
The dead are coming back again, the years are rolled away
In Sherwood, in Sherwood, about the break of day.

Softly over Sherwood the south wind blows.
All the heart of England hid in every rose
Hears across the greenwood the sunny whisper leap,
Sherwood in the red dawn, is Robin Hood asleep?

Hark, the voice of England wakes him as of old
And, shattering the silence with a cry of brighter gold,
Bugles in the greenwood echo from the steep,
Sherwood in the red dawn, is Robin Hood asleep?

Where the deer are gliding down the shadowy glen
All across the glades of fern he calls his merry men —
Doublets of the Lincoln green glancing through the May
In Sherwood, in Sherwood, about the break of day —

Calls them and they answer; from aisles of oak and ash
Rings the *Follow! Follow!* and the boughs begin to crash,
The ferns begin to flutter and the flowers begin to fly,
And through the crimson dawning the robber band goes by.

Robin! Robin! Robin! All his merry thieves
Answer as the bugle-note shivers through the leaves,
Calling as he used to call, faint and far away,
In Sherwood, in Sherwood, about the break of day.

—Alfred Noyes

♪ THOMAS RYMER

True Thomas lay oer yond grassy bank,
  And he beheld a ladie gay,
A ladie that was brisk and bold,
  Come riding oer the fernie brae.

Her skirt was of the grass-green silk,
  Her mantle of the velvet fine,
At ilka tett of her horse's mane
  Hung fifty silver bells and nine.

True Thomas he took off his hat,
  And bowed him low down till his knee:
'All hail, thou mighty Queen of Heaven!
  For your peer on earth I never did see.'

'O no, O no, True Thomas,' she says,
  'That name does not belong to me;
I am but the queen of fair Elfland,
  And I'm come here for to visit thee. . . .

'But ye maun go wi me now, Thomas,
  True Thomas, ye maun go wi me,
For ye maun serve me seven years,
  Thro weel or wae as may chance to be.

'Then harp and carp, Thomas,' she said,
  'Then harp and carp, alang wi me;
But it will be seven years and a day
  Till ye win back to yere ain countrie.'

ilka tett: each lock or knot of hair.
carp: sing.

She turned about her milk-white steed,
  And took True Thomas up behind,
And aye wheneer her bridle rang,
  The steed flew swifter than the wind.

For forty days and forty nights
  He wade thro red blude to the knee,
And he saw neither sun nor moon,
  But heard the roaring of the sea.

Oh they rade on and further on.
  Until they came to a garden green:
'Light down, light down, ye ladie free,
  Some of that fruit let me pull to thee.'

'O no, O no, True Thomas,' she says,
  'That fruit maun not be touched by thee,
For a' the plagues that are in hell
  Light on the fruit of this countrie.

'But I have a loaf here in my lap,
  Likewise a bottle of claret wine,
And now ere we go farther on,
  We'll rest a while, and ye may dine.'

When he had eaten and drunk his fill: —
  'Lay down your head upon my knee,'
The ladie sayd, 'ere we climb yon hill
  And I will show you fairlies three.

'O see not ye yon narrow road,
  So thick beset wi thorns and briers?
That is the path of righteousness,
  Tho after it but few enquires.

'And see not ye that braid braid road,
   That lies across yon lillie leven?
That is the path of wickedness,
   Tho some call it the road to heaven.

'And see not ye that bonny road,
   Which winds about the fernie brae?
That is the road to fair Elfland,
   Where you and I this night maun gae.

'But Thomas, ye maun hold your tongue,
   Whatever you may hear or see,
For gin ae word you should chance to speak,
   You will neer get back to your ain countrie.'

He has gotten a coat of the even cloth,
   And a pair of shoes of velvet green,
And till seven years were past and gone
   True Thomas on earth was never seen.

leven: lawn or grass land.
brae: hill.

— *Traditional: Scots*

THE WEE WEE MAN

As I was walking mine alane
    Atween a water and a wa',
There I spied a wee wee man,
    And he was the least that ere I saw.

His legs were scarce a shathmont's length,
    And thick and thimber was his thie;
Atween his brows there was a span,
    And atween his shoulders there was three.

He's taen and flung a meikle stane,
    And he flang it far as I could see;
Though I had been a Wallace wight
    I couldna liften 't to my knee.

'O wee wee man, but ye be strang!
    O tell me where your dwelling be?'
'My dwelling's down by yon bonny bower;
    Fair lady, come wi' me and see.'

On we lap, and awa' we rade,
    Till we came to yon bonny green;
We lighted down to bait our steed,
    And out there came a lady sheen;

Wi' four and twenty at her back
    A' comely clad in glisterin' green;
Tho' the King of Scotland had been there,
    The warst o' them might ha' been his queen.

shathmont: measure from the point of the extended thumb to the extremity of the palm — about six inches.
thimber: stout.
thie: thigh.
lap: leapt.
sheen: shining, beautiful.

On we lap, and awa' we rade,
  Till we came to a bonny ha';
The roof was o' the beaten gowd,
  And the floor was o' the cristal a'.

When we came to the stair-foot,
  Ladies were dancing jimp and sma',
But in the twinkling of an eie
  My wee wee man was clean awa'.

Out gat the lights, on came the mist,
  Ladies nor mannie mair could I see;
I turned about, and gae a look
  Just at the foot o' Benachie.

— *Traditional: Scots*

THE FIDDLING LAD

'There'll be no roof to shelter you;
  You'll have no where to lay your head.
And who will get your bread for you?
  Star-dust pays for no man's bread.
    So, Jacky, give me your fiddle
    If ever you mean to thrive.'

'I'll have the skies to shelter me,
  The green grass it shall be my bed,
And happen I'll find somewhere for me
  A sup of drink, a bit of bread;
    And I'll not give my fiddle
    To any man alive.'

142

And it's out he went across the wold,
 His fiddle tucked beneath his chin,
And (golden bow on silver strings)
 Smiling he fiddled the twilight in;

And fiddled in the frosty moon,
 And all the stars of the Milky Way,
And fiddled low through the dark of dawn,
 And laughed and fiddled in the day.

But oh, he had no bite nor sup,
 And oh, the winds blew stark and cold,
And when he dropped on his grass-green bed
 It's long he slept in the open wold.

They digged his grave and, 'There,' they said,
 'He's got more land than ever he had,
And well it will keep him held and housed,
 The feckless bit of a fiddling lad.'

And it's out he's stepped across the wold
 His fiddle tucked beneath his chin —
A wavering shape in the wavering light,
 Smiling he fiddles the twilight in,

And fiddles in the frosty moon,
 And all the stars of the Milky Way,
And fiddles now through the dark of dawn,
 And laughs and fiddles in the day.

He needeth not or bit or sup,
 The winds of night he need not fear,
And (bow of gold on silver strings)
 It's all the people turn to hear.

'Oh never,' it's all the people cry,
  'Came such sweet sounds from mortal hand';
And, 'Listen,' they say, 'it's some ghostly boy
  That goes a-fiddling through the land.

Hark you! It's night comes slipping in, —
  The moon and the stars that tread the sky;
And there's the breath of the world that stops;
  And now with a shout the sun comes by!'

Who heareth him he heedeth not
  But smiles content, the fiddling lad;
He murmurs, 'Oh many's the happy day
  My fiddle and I together have had;
    And could I give my fiddle
    To any man alive?'

                              — *Adelaide Crapsey*

♪ THE WRAGGLE TAGGLE GIPSIES O!

There were three gipsies a-come to my door
  And downstairs ran this a-lady, O!
One sang high and another sang low
  And the other sang bonny, bonny Biscay O!

Then she pull'd off her silk finish'd gown
  And put on hose of leather, O!
The ragged, ragged rags about our door
  She's gone with the wraggle taggle gipsies, O!

It was late last night, when my lord came home,
  Enquiring for his a-lady, O!

144

The servants said on ev'ry hand:
    She's gone with the wraggle taggle gipsies O!

O, saddle to me my milk-white steed,
    Go and fetch me my pony, O!
That I may ride and seek my bride,
    Who is gone with the wraggle taggle gipsies, O!

O he rode high and he rode low,
    He rode through woods and copses too,
Until he came to an open field,
    And there he espied his a-lady, O!

What makes you leave your house and land?
    What makes you leave your money, O?
What makes you leave your new wedded lord,
    To go with the wraggle taggle gipsies, O?

What care I for my house and land?
    What care I for my money, O?
What care I for my new wedded lord?
    I'm off with the wraggle taggle gipsies, O!

Last night you slept on a goose-feather bed,
    With the sheet turn'd down so bravely, O!
And tonight you'll sleep in a cold open field,
    Along with the wraggle taggle gipsies, O!

What care I for a goose-feather bed,
    With the sheet turn'd down so bravely, O?
For tonight I shall sleep in a cold open field,
    Along with the wraggle taggle gipsies, O!

                — *Traditional: English*

♭ GREEN BROOM

There was an old man lived out in the wood,
　His trade was a-cutting of Broom, green Broom;
He had but one son without thrift, without good,
　Who lay in his bed till 'twas noon, bright noon.

The old man awoke, one morning and spoke,
　He swore he would fire the room, that room,
If his John would not rise and open his eyes,
　And away to the wood to cut Broom, green Broom.

So Johnny arose, and he slipped on his clothes,
　And away to the wood to cut Broom, green Broom,
He sharpened his knives, for once he contrives
　To cut a great bundle of Broom, green Broom.

When Johnny passed under a lady's fine house,
　Passed under a lady's fine room, fine room,
She called to her maid, 'Go fetch me,' she said,
　'Go fetch me the boy that sells Broom, green Broom.'

When Johnny came in to the lady's fine house,
　And stood in the lady's fine room, fine room;
'Young Johnny,' she said, 'Will you give up your trade,
　And marry a lady in bloom, full bloom?'

Johnny gave his consent, and to church they both went,
　And he wedded the lady in bloom, full bloom,
At market and fair, all folks do declare,
　There is none like the Boy that sold Broom, green Broom.

— Unknown

♪ THE PLOUGHBOY IN LUCK

My daddy is dead, but I can't tell you how;
He left me six horses to follow the plough;
    With my whim wham waddle ho!
    Strim stram straddle ho!
    Bubble ho! pretty boy over the brow.

I sold my six horses to buy me a cow;
And wasn't that a pretty thing to follow the plough?
    With my whim wham waddle ho!
    Strim stram straddle ho!
    Bubble ho! pretty boy over the brow.

I sold my cow to buy me a calf,
For I never made a bargain but I lost the best half.
    With my whim wham waddle ho!
    Strim stram straddle ho!
    Bubble ho! pretty boy over the brow.

I sold my calf to buy me a cat,
To sit down before the fire to warm her pretty back,
    With my whim wham waddle ho!
    Strim stram straddle ho!
    Bubble ho! pretty boy over the brow.

I sold my cat to buy me a mouse,
But she took fire in her tail and so burnt up my house,
    With my whim wham waddle ho!
    Strim stram straddle ho!
    Bubble ho! pretty boy over the brow.

— Traditional: English

JOHN AND HIS MARE

John and his mare a journey went,
Humble, dumble, derry derry dee;
They travelled slow, by joint consent,
Tweedle, tweedle, tweedle, twinery.

They travelled near a hundred miles,
Humble, dumble, derry derry dee;
The mare jumped over all the stiles,
Tweedle, tweedle, tweedle, twinery.

It rained and blew as night came on,
Humble, dumble, derry derry dee;
Said John, 'I wish we were at home,'
Tweedle, tweedle, tweedle, twinery.

Then said the mare, 'What shall we do?'
Humble, dumble, derry derry dee;
'Good Master, I have lost a shoe.'
Tweedle, tweedle, tweedle, twinery.

'Alack!' said John, 'where can we stop?
Humble, dumble, derry derry dee.
I do not see a blacksmith's shop.'
Tweedle, tweedle, tweedle, twinery.

At length they came to a great hall,
Humble, dumble, derry derry dee,
Where John did loudly knock and call,
Tweedle, tweedle, tweedle, twinery.

The King came out all dressed so gay,
Humble, dumble, derry derry dee,

And begged to know what he'd to say.
Tweedle, tweedle, tweedle, twinery.

Says John, 'I'm wet, Sir, to the skin.'
Humble, dumble, derry derry dee.
Then said the King, 'Pray, sir, step in.'
Tweedle, tweedle, tweedle, twinery.

The King brought a dry shirt for John,
Humble, dumble, derry derry dee,
And helped him to put it on.
Tweedle, tweedle, tweedle, twinery.

He introduced him to the Queen,
Humble, dumble, derry derry dee,
As fair a dame as e'er was seen.
Tweedle, tweedle, tweedle, twinery.

He gave him supper and a bed,
Humble, dumble, derry derry dee,
And ordered that his horse be fed.
Tweedle, tweedle, tweedle, twinery.

So well did John behave him there,
Humble, dumble, derry derry dee,
The King and Queen made him Lord Mayor.
Tweedle, tweedle, tweedle, twinery.

And now John's got a coach and four,
Humble, dumble, derry derry dee,
I'll end my song, and sing no more
Tweedle, tweedle, tweedle, twinery.

— *Traditional: English*

♪ WIDDICOMBE FAIR

'Tom Pearse, Tom Pearse, lend me your gray mare,
  All along, down along, out along, lee.
For I want for to go to Widdicombe Fair,
  Wi' Bill Brewer, Jan Stewer, Peter Gurney, Peter Davy,
  Dan'l Whiddon, Harry Hawk,
Old Uncle Tom Cobleigh and all.'
  Old Uncle Tom Cobleigh and all.

'And when shall I see again my gray mare?' —
  All along, down along, out along, lee.
'By Friday soon, or Saturday noon,
  Wi' Bill Brewer, Jan Stewer, Peter Gurney, Peter Davy,
  Dan'l Whiddon, Harry Hawk,
Old Uncle Tom Cobleigh and all.'
  Old Uncle Tom Cobleigh and all.

Then Friday came and Saturday noon,
  All along, down along, out along, lee.
But Tom Pearse's old mare hath not trotted home,
  Wi' Bill Brewer, Jan Stewer, Peter Gurney, Peter Davy,
  Dan'l Whiddon, Harry Hawk,
Old Uncle Tom Cobleigh and all.
  Old Uncle Tom Cobleigh and all.

So Tom Pearse he got up to the top o' the hill,
  All along, down along, out along, lee.
And he sees his old mare down a-making her will,
  Wi' Bill Brewer, Jan Stewer, Peter Gurney, Peter Davy,
  Dan'l Whiddon, Harry Hawk,
Old Uncle Tom Cobleigh and all.
  Old Uncle Tom Cobleigh and all.

150

So Tom Pearse's old mare her took sick and her died,
  All along, down along, out along, lee.
And Tom he sat down on a stone, and he cried
  Wi' Bill Brewer, Jan Stewer, Peter Gurney, Peter Davy,
  Dan'l Whiddon, Harry Hawk,
Old Uncle Tom Cobleigh and all.
  Old Uncle Tom Cobleigh and all.

But this isn't the end o' this shocking affair,
  All along, down along, out along, lee.
Nor, though they be dead, of the horrid career
  Of Bill Brewer, Jan Stewer, Peter Gurney, Peter Davy,
  Dan'l Whiddon, Harry Hawk,
Old Uncle Tom Cobleigh and all.
  Old Uncle Tom Cobleigh and all.

When the wind whistles cold on the moor of a night,
  All along, down along, out along, lee.
Tom Pearse's old mare doth appear, gashly white,
  Wi' Bill Brewer, Jan Stewer, Peter Gurney, Peter Davy,
  Dan'l Whiddon, Harry Hawk,
Old Uncle Tom Cobleigh and all.
  Old Uncle Tom Cobleigh and all.

And all the long night he heard skirling and groans,
  All along, down along, out along, lee.
From Tom Pearse's old mare in her rattling bones,
  And from Bill Brewer, Jan Stewer, Peter Gurney, Peter
    Davy,
  Dan'l Whiddon, Harry Hawk,
Old Uncle Tom Cobleigh and all.
  OLD UNCLE TOM COBLEIGH AND ALL.

— Traditional: English

♪ THE FARMER'S CURST WIFE

There was an old farmer went out for to plow,
  With a new sing naggle sing new,
There was an old farmer went out for to plow,
He hitched up an ox and an ass and a cow,
  With a new sing naggle sing new, new, new,
  A new sing naggle sing new.

The devil flew by with a flickety-flack,
  With a new sing naggle sing new,
The devil flew by with a flickety-flack,
He carried a pitch-fork wrapped up in a sack,
  With a new sing naggle sing new, new, new,
  A new sing naggle sing new.

The old farmer droppèd his lines and he run,
'The devil's a-lookin' for my oldest son.'

'I don't want your son nor your daughter fair,
But your old scoldin' wife what's lost all of her hair.'

So sayin' he harvest her up on his back,
And he left like a pedlar a-totin' his pack.

He toted her down to the gates of hell,
Said, 'Blow up the fire, boys, we'll roast this one well.'

Seven small devils came rattlin' their chains,
She handled a poker and mellered their brains.

The other small devil looked over the wall,
Said, 'Take her back, daddy, she'll murder us all.'

He harvest her up on his poor old tired back,
And he left like a pedlar a-totin' his pack.

Seven years goin' and six comin' back,
She asked for the corn-pone she left in the crack.

'Oh, what I can do now the devil won't tell,
    With a new sing naggle sing new,
Oh what I can do now the devil won't tell,
I ain't fit for heaven and I'm too mean for hell,
    With a new sing naggle sing new, new, new,
    A new sing naggle sing new.'

— Traditional: American

Collected by *John Jacob Niles*

♩ THERE WAS AN OLD WOMAN

There was an old woman and she had a little pig,
    Go find my true love;
There was an old woman and she had a little pig,
Didn't cost so much 'cause it wasn't very big,
    Go find my true love in some lonesome valley.

Now this little pig it did a heap of harm,
    Go find my true love;
Now this little pig it did a heap of harm,
Making little tracks all around of the barn.
    Go find my true love in some lonesome valley.

Now this little pig it died in its bed
All because they didn't give it no bread.

Now the old woman's husband died of grief,
Wasn't that a sad relief?

Then the old woman wept and she sobbed and she cried,
And she too then laid down and died.

And then they laid 'em out all cold and dead,
    Go find my true love;
And then they laid 'em out all cold and dead,
With the pig at the foot and the husband at the head,
    Go find my true love in some lonesome valley.

— *Traditional: American*

Collected by *John Jacob Niles*

154

LITTLE DAME CRUMP

Oh, little Dame Crump with her little hair broom
　One morning was sweeping her little bed room
When casting her little gray eyes on the ground
　In a sly little corner a penny she found.

'Odd-dobbs,' cried the maid, and she starts with surprise,
　'How lucky I am; bless me heart, what a prize!
'To the market I'll go and a pig I will buy
　'And little John Gubbins shall build him a sty!'

So she washed her face clean and put on her gown,
　And locked up her house and started for town.
To market she went and a bargain she made,
　And for little white piggie a penny she paid.

Now the bargain was made she was puzzled to know
　How they both would get home, as the pig would not go.
So fearing that piggie might play her a trick,
　She drove him along with a little crab stick.

Piggie ran till he came to the foot of a hill
　Where a little bridge crosses a stream from a mill,
There he grunted and squealed and no further would go.
　Oh, fie, little piggie, to serve poor dame so!

She went into the mill and borrowed a sack
　Popped in the pig and took him on her back.
Piggie squealed to get out, but the little dame said,
　'If you can't go by fair means, then you must be made.'

She soon to the end of the journey did come,
　She was mightily pleased to get piggie home.

She carried him right to his nice little sty,
    And made him a bed of straw clean and dry.

With a handful of pease poor piggie she fed;
    She popped on her nightcap and hopped into bed.
Having first said her prayers, she blew out the light,
    And being quite tired, we'll bid her goodnight.

— Traditional: English

♪ THE LITTLE DISASTER

Once there lived a little man
Where a little river ran,
And he had a little farm and little dairy O!
And he had a little plough,
And he had a dappled cow,
Which he often called his pretty little fairy O!

And his dog he called Fidelle,
For he loved his master well;
And he had a little pony for his pleasure O!
In a sty not very big,
He'd a frisky little pig,
Which he often called his little piggy treasure O!

Once his little maiden, Ann,
With her pretty little can,
Went a-milking when the morning sun was beaming O!
When she fell, I don't know how,
But she tumbled o'er the plough,
And the cow was quite astonished at her screaming O!

Little maid cried out in vain
While the milk ran o'er the plain,
Little pig ran grunting after it so gaily O!
While the little dog behind
For a share was much inclined,
So he pulled back squeaking piggy by the taily O!

Such a clatter now began
As alarmed the little man,
Who came capering from out his little stable O!
Pony trod on doggy's toes,
Doggy snapped at piggy's nose,
Piggy made as great a noise as he was able O!

Then to make the story short,
Little pony with a snort
Lifted up his little heels so clever O!
And the man he tumbled down
And he nearly cracked his crown,
And this only made the matter worse than ever O!

— Traditional: English

157

♪ JOHN GILPIN

John Gilpin was a citizen
   Of credit and renown,
A train-band captain eke was he
   Of famous London Town.

John Gilpin's spouse said to her dear,
   'Though wedded we have been
These twice ten tedious years, yet we
   No holiday have seen.

'Tomorrow is our wedding-day,
   And we will then repair
Unto the Bell at Edmonton,
   All in a chaise and pair.

'My sister and my sister's child,
   Myself, and children three,
Will fill the chaise; so you must ride
   On horseback after we.'

He soon replied, 'I do admire
   Of womankind but one,
And you are she, my dearest dear,
   Therefore it shall be done.

'I am a linen-draper bold,
   As all the world doth know,
And my good friend, the Calender,
   Will lend his horse to go.'

Quoth Mrs. Gilpin, 'That's well said;
   And for that wine is dear,

We will be furnish'd with our own,
　　Which is both bright and clear.'

John Gilpin kiss'd his loving wife;
　　O'erjoyed was he to find
That, though on pleasure she was bent,
　　She had a frugal mind.

The morning came, the chaise was brought,
　　But yet was not allowed
To drive up to the door, lest all
　　Should say that she was proud.

So three doors off the chaise was stay'd,
　　Where they did all get in,
Six precious souls, and all agog
　　To dash through thick and thin.

Smack went the whip, round went the wheels,
　　Were never folk so glad;
The stones did rattle underneath,
　　As if Cheapside were mad.

John Gilpin, at his horse's side,
　　Seiz'd fast the flowing mane,
And up he got, in haste to ride,
　　But soon came down again;

For saddle-tree scarce reach'd had he,
　　His journey to begin,
When, turning round his head, he saw
　　Three customers come in.

So down he came; for loss of time,
  Although it grieved him sore,
Yet loss of pence, full well he knew,
  Would trouble him much more.

'Twas long before the customers
  Were suited to their mind,
When Betty, screaming, came downstairs,
  'The wine is left behind!'

'Good lack!' quoth he, 'Yet bring it me,
  My leathern belt likewise,
In which I bear my trusty sword
  When I do exercise.'

Now Mistress Gilpin, (careful soul!)
  Had two stone-bottles found,
To hold the liquor that she loved,
  And keep it safe and sound.

Each bottle had a curling ear,
  Through which the belt he drew,
And hung a bottle on each side,
  To make his balance true.

Then over all, that he might be
  Equipp'd from top to toe,
His long red cloak, well brush'd and neat,
  He manfully did throw.

Now see him mounted once again
  Upon his nimble steed,
Full slowly pacing o'er the stones,
  With caution and good heed.

But finding soon a smoother road
  Beneath his well-shod feet,
The snorting beast began to trot,
  Which gall'd him in his seat.

So, 'Fair and softly,' John he cried,
  But John he cried in vain;
That trot became a gallop soon,
  In spite of curb and rein.

So stooping down, as needs he must
  Who cannot sit upright,
He grasp'd the mane with both his hands,
  And eke, with all his might.

His horse, who never in that sort
  Had handled been before,
What thing upon his back had got
  Did wonder more and more.

Away went Gilpin, neck or nought;
  Away went hat and wig;
He little dreamt, when he set out,
  Of running such a rig.

The wind did blow, the cloak did fly,
  Like streamer long and gay,
Till loop and button failing both,
  At last it flew away.

Then might all people well discern
  The bottles he had slung;
A bottle swinging at each side,
  As hath been said or sung.

The dogs did bark, the children scream'd,
  Up flew the windows all;
And every soul cried out, — 'Well done!'
  As loud as he could bawl.

Away went Gilpin — who but he?
  His fame soon spread around,
'He carries weight! He rides a race!
  'Tis for a thousand pound!'

And still as fast as he drew near,
  'Twas wonderful to view
How in a trice the turnpike men
  Their gates wide open threw.

And now, as he went bowing down
  His reeking head full low,
The bottles twain behind his back
  Were shatter'd at a blow.

Down ran the wine into the road,
  Most piteous to be seen,
Which made his horse's flanks to smoke
  As they had basted been.

But still he seemed to carry weight,
  With leathern girdle braced;
For all might see the bottle necks
  Still dangling at his waist.

Thus all through merry Islington
  These gambols he did play,
Until he came unto the Wash
  Of Edmonton so gay;

And there he threw the Wash about
  On both sides of the way,
Just like unto a trundling mop,
  Or a wild goose at play.

At Edmonton his loving wife
  From the balcony spied
Her tender husband, wondering much
  To see how he did ride.

'Stop, stop, John Gilpin! — Here's the house' —
  They all at once did cry;
'The dinner waits, and we are tired';
  Said Gilpin, 'So am I!'

But yet his horse was not a whit
  Inclin'd to tarry there;
For why? his owner had a house
  Full ten miles off, at Ware.

So like an arrow swift he flew,
  Shot by an archer strong;
So did he fly — which brings me to
  The middle of my song.

Away went Gilpin, out of breath,
  And sore against his will,
Till, at his friend the Calender's,
  His horse at last stood still.

The Calender, amazed to see
  His neighbour in such trim,
Laid down his pipe, flew to the gate,
  And thus accosted him.

'What news? what news? your tidings tell;
    Tell me you must and shall —
Say, why bare-headed you are come,
    Or why you come at all?'

Now Gilpin had a pleasant wit,
    And loved a timely joke;
And thus, unto the Calender,
    In merry guise he spoke:

'I came because your horse would come;
    And, if I well forebode,
My hat and wig will soon be here,
    They are upon the road.'

The Calender, right glad to find
    His friend in merry pin,
Return'd him not a single word,
    But to the house went in;

Whence straight he came, with hat and wig,
    A wig that flow'd behind;
A hat not much the worse for wear,
    Each comely in its kind.

He held them up, and in his turn
    Thus showed his ready wit:
'My head is twice as big as yours,
    They therefore needs must fit.

'But let me scrape the dust away,
    That hangs upon your face;
And stop and eat, for well you may
    Be in a hungry case.'

Said John, 'It is my wedding-day,
    And all the world will stare,
If wife should dine at Edmonton,
    And I should dine at Ware.'

So, turning to his horse, he said,
    'I am in haste to dine;
'Twas for your pleasure you came here,
    You shall go back for mine.'

Ah, luckless speech, and bootless boast!
    For which he paid full dear;
For, while he spake, a braying ass
    Did sing most loud and clear;

Whereat his horse did snort, as he
    Had heard a lion roar,
And gallop'd off with all his might,
    As he had done before.

Away went Gilpin, and away
    Went Gilpin's hat and wig;
He lost them sooner than at first,
    For why? — they were too big.

Now Mistress Gilpin, when she saw
    Her husband posting down
Into the country far away,
    She pull'd out half a crown;

And thus unto the youth she said,
    That drove them to the Bell,
'This shall be yours, when you bring back
    My husband safe and well.'

The youth did ride, and soon did meet
  John coming back amain;
Whom in a trice he tried to stop,
  By catching at his rein;

But not performing what he meant,
  And gladly would have done,
The frightened horse he frightened more,
  And made him faster run.

Away went Gilpin, and away
  Went postboy at his heels,
The postboy's horse right glad to miss
  The rumbling of the wheels.

Six gentlemen upon the road
  Thus seeing Gilpin fly,
With postboy scampering in the rear,
  They rais'd a hue and cry:

'Stop thief! — stop thief! a highwayman!'
  Not one of them was mute;
And all and each that pass'd that way
  Did join in the pursuit.

And now the turnpike gates again
  Flew open in short space;
The toll-men, thinking as before
  That Gilpin rode a race.

And so he did, and won it too,
  For he got first to town;
Nor stopp'd till where he had got up
  He did again get down.

Now let us sing, Long live the King,
  And Gilpin, long live he;
And, when he next doth ride abroad,
  May I be there to see.

                    — William Cowper

THE DEACON'S MASTERPIECE

Have you heard of the wonderful one-hoss shay,
That was built in such a logical way
It ran a hundred years to a day,
And then, of a sudden, it — ah, but stay,
I'll tell you what happened without delay:
Scaring the parson into fits,
Frightening people out of their wits —
Have you ever heard of that, I say?

Seventeen hundred and fifty-five;
Georgius Secundus was then alive, —
Snuffy old drone from the German hive.
That was the year when Lisbon-town
Saw the earth open and gulp her down,
And Braddock's army was done so brown,
Left without a scalp to its crown.
It was the terrible Earthquake day
That the Deacon finished the one-hoss shay.

Now in building chaises, I tell you what,
There is always *somewhere* a weakest spot, —
In hub, tire, felloe, in spring or thill,
In panel, or cross-bar, or floor, or sill,
In screw, bolt, thoroughbrace, — lurking still,
Find it somewhere you must and will, —
Above or below, or within or without, —
And that's the reason, beyond a doubt,
That a chaise *breaks down,* but doesn't *wear out.*

But the Deacon swore (as Deacons do,
With an 'I dew vum,' or an 'I tell *yeou*')

He would build one shay to beat the taown
'N' the keounty 'n' all the kentry raoun';
It should be so built that it couldn't break daown:
'Fur,' said the Deacon, ''t's mighty plain
Thut the weakes' place mus' stan' the strain;
'N' the way t' fix it, uz I maintain,
                    Is only jest
T' make that place uz strong uz the rest.'

So the Deacon inquired of the village folk
Where he could find the strongest oak,
That couldn't be split nor bent nor broke, —
That was for spokes and floor and sills;
He sent for lancewood to make the thills;
The crossbars were ash, from the straightest trees;
The panels of white-wood, that cuts like cheese,
But lasts like iron for things like these;
The hubs of logs from the 'Settler's ellum,'
Last of its timber, — they couldn't sell 'em, —
Never an axe had seen their chips,
And the wedges flew from between their lips,
Their blunt ends frizzled like celery-tips;
Step and prop-iron, bolt and screw,
Spring, tire, axle, and linch-pin too,
Steel of the finest, bright and blue;
Thoroughbrace bison-skin, thick and wide;
Boot, top, dasher, from tough old hide
Found in the pit when the tanner died.
That was the way he 'put her through.'
'There!' said the Deacon, 'Naow she'll dew!'

Do! I tell you, I rather guess
She was a wonder, and nothing less!

Colts grew horses, beards turned gray,
Deacon and deaconess dropped away,
Children and grandchildren — where were they?
But there stood the stout old one-hoss shay
As fresh as on Lisbon-earthquake day!

Eighteen hundred; — it came and found
The Deacon's masterpiece strong and sound.
Eighteen hundred increased by ten; —
'Hahnsum kerridge' they called it then.
Eighteen hundred and twenty came; —
Running as usual; much the same.
Thirty and forty at last arrive,
And then come fifty, and *fifty-five*.

Little of all we value here
Wakes on the morn of its hundredth year
Without both feeling and looking queer.
In fact, there's nothing that keeps its youth,
So far as I know, but a tree and truth.
(This is a moral that runs at large;
Take it. — You're welcome. — No extra charge.)

First of November, — the Earthquake day, —
There are traces of age in the one-hoss shay,
A general flavour of mild decay,
But nothing local, as one may say.
There couldn't be, — for the Deacon's art
Had made it so like in every part
That there wasn't a chance for one to start.
For the wheels were just as strong as the thills,
And the floor was just as strong as the sills,
And the panels just as strong as the floor,
And the whipple-tree neither less nor more,

170

And the back cross-bar as strong as the fore,
And spring and axle and hub *encore.*
And yet, as a *whole,* it is past a doubt
In another hour it will be *worn out!*

First of November, 'Fifty-five!
This morning the parson takes a drive.
Now, small boys, get out of the way!
Here comes the wonderful one-hoss shay,
Drawn by a rat-tailed, ewe-necked bay.
'Huddup!' said the parson. — Off went they.

The parson was working his Sunday text, —
Had got to *fifthly,* and stopped perplexed
At what the — Moses — was coming next.
All at once the horse stood still,
Close by the meet'n'-house on the hill.
First a shiver, and then a thrill,
Then something decidedly like a spill,
And the parson was sitting upon a rock,
At half-past nine by the meet'n'-house clock, —
Just the hour of the Earthquake shock!
What do you think the parson found,
When he got up and stared around?
The poor old chaise in a heap or mound,
As if it had been to the mill and ground!
You see, of course, if you're not a dunce,
How it went to pieces all at once, —
All at once, and nothing first,
Just as bubbles do when they burst.

End of the wonderful one-hoss shay.
Logic is logic. That's all I say.

— Oliver Wendell Holmes

♩ JOHN HENRY

When John Henry was about three days old,
  A-sittin' on his pappy's knee,
He gave-a one long loud and-a lonesome cry,
  Said, 'Dat hammer'll be the death of me.'

Now John Henry said to his Captain one day,
  'A man ain't nothing but a man,
But before I'll be governed by an ole steam drill
  I'll die with my hammer in my hand.'

Now John Henry swung his hammer around of his head,
  And brought his hammer down on the ground.
A man in Chatanooga, two hundred miles away,
  Heard an awful rumbling sound.

Now John Henry had a pretty little gal,
  Her name was Polly Anne.
When John Henry was sick and a-layin' on his bed,
  Polly drove steel like a man.

When John Henry died, they wasn't no box
  Big enough to hold his bones,
So they buried him in a box-car deep in the ground,
  And let two mountains be his grave-stones.

— *Traditional: American*

Collected by *John Jacob Niles*

FORTY SINGING SEAMEN

Across the seas of Wonderland to Mogadore we plodded,
Forty singing seamen in an old black barque,
And we landed in the twilight where a Polyphemus nodded,
With his battered moon-eye winking red and yellow
    through the dark!
  For his eye was growing mellow,
  Rich and ripe and red and yellow,
As was time, since old Ulysses made him bellow in the dark!
Since Ulysses bunged his eye up with a pine-torch in the
    dark!

Were they mountains in the gloaming or the giant's ugly
    shoulders
Just beneath the rolling eye-ball, with its bleared and
    vinous glow,
Red and yellow o'er the purple of the pines among the
    boulders
And the shaggy horror brooding on the sullen slopes below,
  Were they pines among the boulders
  Or the hair upon his shoulders?
We were only simple seamen, so of course we didn't know.
We were simple singing seamen, so of course we couldn't
    know.

So we crossed a plain of poppies, and we came upon a
    fountain
Not of water, but of jewels, like a spray of leaping fire;
And behind it, in an emerald glade, beneath a golden
    mountain
There stood a crystal palace, for a sailor to admire;
  For a troop of ghosts came round us,
  Which with leaves of bay they crowned us,

Then with grog they well nigh drowned us, to the depth
    of our desire!
And 'twas very friendly of them, as a sailor can admire!

There was music all about us, we were growing quite
    forgetful
We were only singing seamen from the dirt of London-
    town,
Though the nectar that we swallowed seemed to vanish half
    regretful
As if it wasn't good enough to take such vittles down,
    When we saw a sudden figure,
    Tall and black as any nigger,
Like the devil — only bigger — drawing near us with a
    frown!
Like the devil — but much bigger — and he wore a golden
    crown!

And 'What's all this?' he growls at us! With dignity we
    chaunted,
'Forty singing seamen, sir, as won't be put upon!'
'What? Englishmen?' he cries, 'Well, if ye don't mind being
    haunted,
Faith, you're welcome to my palace; I'm the famous Prester
    John!
    Will ye walk into my palace?
    I don't bear 'ee any malice!
One and all ye shall be welcome in the halls of Prester
    John!'
So we walked into the palace and the halls of Prester John!

Now the door was one great diamond and the hall a hollow
    ruby —
Big as Beachy Head, my lads, nay, bigger by a half!

And I sees the mate wi' mouth agape, a-staring like a booby,
And the skipper close behind him, with his tongue out like
a calf!
  Now the way to take it rightly
  Was to walk along politely
Just as if you didn't notice — so I couldn't help but laugh!
For they both forgot their manners and the crew was bound
to laugh!

But he took us through his palace, and, my lads, as I'm a
sinner,
We walked into an opal like a sunset-coloured cloud —
'My dining room,' he says, and, quick as light, we saw a
dinner
Spread before us by the fingers of a hidden fairy crowd;
  And the skipper, swaying gently
  After dinner, murmurs faintly,
'I looks to-wards you, Prester John, you've done us very
proud!'
And he drank his health with honours, for he *done* us *very*
proud!

Then he walks us to his gardens where we sees a feathered
demon
Very splendid and important on a sort of spicy tree!
'That's the Phoenix,' whispers Prester, 'which all eddicated
seamen
Knows the only one existent, and *he's* waiting for to flee!
  When his hundred years expire
  Then he'll set hisself a-fire
And another from his ashes rise most beautiful to see!
With wings of rose and emerald, most beautiful to see!'

Then he says, 'In yonder forest there's a little silver river
And whosoever drinks of it, his youth will never die!
The centuries go by, but Prester John endures forever
With his music in the mountains and his magic on the sky!
    While *your* hearts are growing colder,
    While your world is growing older,
There's a magic in the distance, where the sea-line meets
      the sky.
It shall call to singing seamen till the fount o' song is dry!'

So we thought we'd up and seek it, but that forest fair
      defied us, —
First a crimson leopard laughed at us most horrible to see,
Then a sea-green lion came and sniffed and licked his chops
      and eyed us,
While a red and yellow unicorn was dancing round a tree!
    We was trying to look thinner,
    Which was hard, because our dinner
Must ha' made us very tempting to a cat o' high degree!
Must ha' made us very tempting to the whole menarjeree!

So we scuttled from that forest and across the poppy
      meadows
Where the awful shaggy horror brooded o'er us in the dark!
And we pushes out from shore again a-jumping at our
      shadows
And pulls away most joyful to the old black barque!
    And home again we plodded
    While the Polyphemus nodded
With his battered moon-eye winking red and yellow
      through the dark.
Oh, the moon above the mountains red and yellow through
      the dark!

176

Across the seas of Wonderland to London-town we
  blundered,
Forty singing seamen as was puzzled for to know
If the vision that we saw was caused by — here again we
  pondered —
A tipple in a vision forty thousand years ago.
  Could the grog we *dreamt* we swallowed
  Make us *dream* of all that followed?
We were only simple seamen, so of course we didn't know!
We were simple singing seamen, so of course we could not
  know!

—*Alfred Noyes*

THE BALLAD OF THE OYSTERMAN

It was a tall young oysterman lived by the river-side,
His shop was just upon the bank, his boat was on the tide;
The daughter of a fisherman, that was so straight and slim,
Lived over on the other bank, right opposite to him.

It was the pensive oysterman that saw a lovely maid,
Upon a moonlit evening, a-sitting in the shade;
He saw her wave her handkerchief, as much as if to say,
'I'm wide awake, young oysterman, and all the folks away.'

Then up arose the oysterman, and to himself said he,
'I guess I'll leave the skiff at home, for fear that folks should
    see;
I read it in the story-book, that, for to kiss his dear,
Leander swam the Hellespont, — and I will swim this here.'

And he has leaped into the waves, and crossed the shining
    stream,
And he has clambered up the bank, all in the moonlight
    gleam;
Oh, there were kisses sweet as dew, and words as soft as
    rain, —
But they have heard her father's step, and in he leaps again!

Out spoke the ancient fisherman: 'Oh, what was that, my
    daughter?'
''Twas nothing but a pebble, sir, I threw into the water.'
'And what is that, pray tell me, love, that paddles off so
    fast?'
'It's nothing but a porpoise, sir, that's been a-swimming
    past.'

178

Out spoke the ancient fisherman: 'Now, bring me my
  harpoon!
I'll get into my fishing-boat, and fix the fellow soon.'
Down fell the pretty innocent, as falls a snow-white lamb;
Her hair drooped round her pallid cheeks, like seaweed on
  a clam.

Alas for those two loving ones! She waked not from her
  swound,
And he was taken with a cramp, and in the waves was
  drowned;
But fate has metamorphosed them, in pity of their woe,
And now they keep an oyster-shop for mermaids down
  below.

— *Oliver Wendell Holmes*

♪ THE COASTS OF HIGH BARBARY

Look ahead, look astern, look the weather and the lee.
  Blow high! Blow low! and so sailed we.
I see a wreck to windward and a lofty ship to lee,
  A-sailing down all on the coasts of High Barbary.

'Then hail her,' our captain he called o'er the side,
  Blow high! Blow low! and so sailed we.
'O are you a pirate or a man-o'-war?' cried he.
  A-sailing down all on the coasts of High Barbary.

'O are you a pirate or a man-o'-war?' cried we.
  Blow high! Blow low! and so sailed we.
'O no! I'm not a pirate, but a man-o'-war,' cried he.
  A-sailing down all on the coasts of High Barbary.

'Then back up your topsails and heave your vessel to,'
  Blow high! Blow low! and so sailed we.
'For we have got some letters to be carried home by you.'
  A-sailing down all on the coasts of High Barbary.

'We'll back up our topsails and heave our vessel to,'
  Blow high! Blow low! and so sailed we.
'But only in some harbour and along the side of you.'
  A-sailing down all on the coasts of High Barbary.

For broadside, for broadside, they fought all on the main,
  Blow high! Blow low! and so sailed we.
Until at last the frigate shot the pirate's mast away.
  A-sailing down all on the coasts of High Barbary.

'For quarters, for quarters!' the saucy pirate cried,
  Blow high! Blow low! and so sailed we.

182

The quarters that we showed them was to sink them in the
tide.
A-sailing down all on the coasts of High Barbary.

With cutlass and gun, O we fought for hours three;
Blow high! Blow low! and so sailed we.
The ship it was their coffin, and their grave it was the sea.
A-sailing down all on the coasts of High Barbary.

But, oh, it was a cruel sight, and grievèd us full sore,
Blow high! Blow low! and so sailed we.
To see them all a-drowning as they tried to swim to shore.
A-sailing down all on the coasts of High Barbary.

— *Traditional: English*

♪ THE WEEP-WILLOW TREE

Oh, my father has a fine ship a-sailin' on the sea,
And they call her by the name of the Weep-Willow Tree,
And she sails up and down on the lonesome low,
   And she sails on the lonesome sea,
   And she sails on the lonesome sea.

Now they be another ship and she sails on the sea,
And they call her by the name of the Turkish Piree,
But I fear she will sink the Weep-Willow Tree,
   As she sails on the lonesome sea,
   As she sails on the lonesome sea.

'Twas a sailor, a sailor, who quickly spoke, spake he, sayin':
'Captain, my Captain, what will my prize be,
If I should go sink you the Turkish Piree,
   If I sink her in the lonesome sea,
   If I sink her in the lonesome sea?'

'Oh, I will give you gold and I will give you fee,'
Said the Captain to the sailor of the Weep-Willow Tree,
'And my eldest fairest daughter your sweet bride to be,
   If you sink her in the lonesome sea,
   If you sink her in the lonesome sea.'

Oh, the sailor-man was brave and the sailor-man was bold,
As he augered and he augered through the Turkish Piree's
     hold;
And some did play at cards while some did play melee,
   As they sank in the lonesome sea,
   As they sank in the lonesome sea.

Now the sailor-man crept down and slowly back swam he,
And he swam round the side of the Weep-Willow Tree,
    cryin'
'Help me, my Captain, and come give me my fee,
    Lest I drown in the lonesome sea,
    Lest I drown in the lonesome sea.'

Oh, he swam the tother side of the Weep-Willow Tree,
And he cried, 'O my messmates, pray come and succor me,
'Cause I augered forty holes in the Turkish Piree,
    And I'm sinkin' in the lonesome sea,
    And I'm sinkin' in the lonesome sea.'

Oh, they hauled him o'er the side of the Weep-Willow
    Tree,
And he died on the deck with his messmates three,
And they sewed him in his hammock and they sent him
    out to sea,
    And he sank in the lonesome sea,
    And he sank in the lonesome sea.

— *Traditional: American*

Collected by *John Jacob Niles*

♪ THE WHALE

O 'twas in the year of ninety-four,
And of June the second day,
That our gallant ship her anchor weighed
And from Stromness bore away, — brave boys,
 And from Stromness bore away.

Now Speedicut was our Captain's name,
And our ship the *Lion* bold,
And we were bound to far Greenland,
To the land of ice and cold — brave boys,
 To the land of ice and cold.

And when we came to far Greenland,
And to Greenland cold came we,
Where there's ice and there's snow, and the whalefishes
  blow,
We found all open sea, — brave boys,
 We found all open sea.

Then the mate he climbed to the crow's-nest high,
With his spy-glass in his hand,
'There's a whale, there's a whale, there's a whalefish,' he
  cried,
'And she blows in every span,' — brave boys,
 And she blows in every span.

Our captain stood on his quarter-deck,
And a fine little man was he,

whalefish: the term customarily used by Scottish, Dutch, and German
whalemen — not merely 'whale.'
 span: distance from one rise of the whale to the next.

'Overhaul, overhaul, on your davit tackle fall,
And launch your boats to the sea, — brave boys,
    And launch your boats to the sea.'

Now the boats were launched and the men aboard,
With the whalefish full in view;
Resol-ved were the whole boat's crew
To steer where the whalefish blew, — brave boys,
    To steer where the whalefish blew.

And when we reached that whale, my boys,
He lashed out with his tail,
And we lost a boat and seven good men,
And we never caught that whale, — brave boys,
    We never caught that whale.

Bad news, bad news, to our captain came,
That grieved him very sore.
But when he heard that his cabin-boy was gone,
Why it grieved him ten times more, — brave boys,
    It grieved him ten times more.

O, Greenland is an awful place,
Where the daylight's seldom seen,
Where there's ice, and there's snow, and the whalefishes
    blow,
Then adieu to cold Greenland, — brave boys,
    Adieu to cold Greenland.

— Traditional: British

WINDLASS SONG

Heave at the windlass! — Heave O, cheerly, men!
  Heave all at once, with a will!
    The tide quickly making,
    Our cordage a-creaking,
  The water has put on a frill,
          Heave O!

Fare you well, sweethearts! — Heave O, cheerly, men!
  Fare you well, frolic and sport!
    The good ship all ready,
    Each dog-vane is steady,
  The wind blowing dead out of port,
          Heave O!

Once in blue water — Heave O, cheerly, men!
  Blow it from north or from south;
    She'll stand to it tightly,
    And curtsey politely,
  And carry a bone in her mouth,
          Heave O!

Short cruise or long cruise — Heave O, cheerly, men!
  Jolly Jack Tar thinks it one.
    No latitude dreads he
    Of White, Black, or Red Sea,
  Great icebergs, or tropical sun,
          Heave O!

One other turn, and Heave O, cheerly, men!
  Heave, and good-bye to the shore!
    Our money, how went it?
    We shared it and spent it;
  Next year we'll come back with some more,
          Heave O!

— William Allingham

THE SAILOR'S CONSOLATION

One night came on a hurricane,
   The sea was mountains rolling,
When Barney Buntline turned his quid
   And said to Billy Bowling,
'A strong nor'wester's blowing, Bill;
   Hark! don't ye hear it roar, now?
Lord help 'em, how I pities them
   Unhappy folks on shore now!

'Foolhardy chaps who live in towns,
   What danger they are all in,
And now lie quaking in their beds,
   For fear the roof should fall in;
Poor creatures! how they envies us,
   And wishes, I've a notion,
For our good luck, in such a storm,
   To be upon the ocean!

'And as for them who're out all day
   On business from their houses,
And late at night are coming home,
   To cheer their babes and spouses, —
While you and I, Bill, on the deck
   Are comfortably lying,
My eyes! what tiles and chimney-pots
   About their heads are flying!

'And very often have we heard
   How men are killed and undone
By overturns of carriages,
   By thieves and fires in London;

We know what risks all landsmen run,
   From noblemen to tailors;
Then, Bill, let's us thank Providence
   That you and I are sailors.'

                  — *William Pitt*

THE WRECK OF THE 'JULIE PLANTE'

(A Legend of Lac St. Pierre)

On wan dark night on Lac St. Pierre,
   De win' she blow, blow, blow,
An' de crew of de wood scow 'Julie Plante'
   Got scar't an' run below —
For de win' she blow lak hurricane
   Bimeby she blow some more,
An' de scow bus' up on Lac St. Pierre
   Wan arpent from de shore.

De captinne walk on de fronte deck,
   An' walk de hin' deck too —
He call de crew from up de hole
   He call de cook also.
De cook she's name was Rosie,
   She come from Montreal,
Was chambre maid on lumber barge,
   On de Grande Lachine Canal.

De win' she blow from nor'-eas'-wes',
   De sout' win' she blow too,
W'en Rosie cry, 'Mon cher captinne,
   Mon cher, w'at I shall do?'

Den de captinne t'row de beeg ankerre,
  But still de scow she dreef:
De crew he can't pass on de shore,
  Becos' he los' hees skeef.

De night was dark lak wan black cat,
  De wave run high an' fas',
W'en de captinne tak' de Rosie girl
  An' tie her to de mas'.
Den he also tak' de life preserve,
  An' jomp off on de lak',
An' say, 'Good-bye, ma Rosie dear,
  I go drown for your sak'!'

Nex' morning very early
  'Bout ha'f-pas' two — t'ree — four —
De captinne — scow — an' de poor Rosie
  Was corpses on de shore,
For de win' she blow lak hurricane,
  Bimeby she blow some more,
An' de scow bus' up on Lac St. Pierre,
  Wan arpent from de shore.

Moral

Now all good wood scow sailor man
  Tak' warning by dat storm
An' go an' marry some nice French girl
  An' leev on wan beeg farm.
De win' can blow lak hurricane,
  An' s'pose she blow some more,
You can't get drown' on Lac St. Pierre
  So long you stay on shore.

— *William Henry Drummond*

BIG STEAMERS

(Written 1910)

'Oh, where are you going to, all you Big Steamers,
With England's own coal, up and down the salt seas?'
'We are going to fetch you your bread and your butter,
Your beef, pork, and mutton, eggs, apples and cheese.'

'And where will you fetch it from, all you Big Steamers,
And where shall I write you when you are away?'
'We fetch it from Melbourne, Quebec, and Vancouver.
Address us at Hobart, Hong-kong, and Bombay.'

'But if anything happened to all you Big Steamers,
And suppose you were wrecked up and down the salt sea?'
'Why, you'd have no coffee or bacon for breakfast,
And you'd have no muffins or toast for your tea.'

'Then I'll pray for fine weather for all you Big Steamers
For little blue billows and breezes so soft.'
'Oh, billows and breezes don't bother Big Steamers:
We're iron below and steel-rigging aloft.'

'Then I'll build a new lighthouse for all you Big Steamers
With plenty wise pilots to pilot you through.'
'Oh, the Channel's as bright as a ball-room already,
And pilots are thicker than pilchards at Looe.'

'Then what can I do for you, all you Big Steamers,
Oh, what can I do for your comfort and good?'
'Send out your big warships to watch your big waters,
That no one may stop us from bringing you food.

For the bread that you eat and the biscuits you nibble,
The sweets that you suck and the joints that you carve,
They are brought to you daily by All Us Big Steamers,
And if anyone hinders our coming you'll starve!'

— *Rudyard Kipling*

CARGOES

Quinquireme of Nineveh from distant Ophir
Rowing home to haven in sunny Palestine,
    With a cargo of ivory,
      And apes and peacocks,
Sandalwood, cedarwood, and sweet white wine.

Stately Spanish galleon coming from the Isthmus,
Dipping through the Tropics by the palm-green shores,
    With a cargo of diamonds,
      Emeralds, amethysts,
Topazes, and cinnamon, and gold moidores.

Dirty British coaster with a salt-caked smoke stack
Butting through the Channel in the mad March days,
    With a cargo of Tyne coal,
      Road rail, pig lead,
Firewood, ironware, and cheap tin trays.

— *John Masefield*

TUGS

At noon three English dowagers ride,
Stiff of neck and dignified,
Margaret, Maud and *Mary Blake,*
With servile barges in their wake;
But silhouetted at midnight,
Darkly, by green and crimson light,
Three Nubian queens pass down the Thames,
Statelily with flashing gems.

— *G. Rostrevor Hamilton*

LOST

Desolate and lone
All night long on the lake
Where fog trails and mist creeps,
The whistle of a boat
Calls and cries unendingly,
Like some lost child
In tears and trouble
Hunting the harbor's breast
And the harbor's eyes.

— *Carl Sandburg*

194

THE OLD SHIPS

I have seen old ships sail like swans asleep
Beyond the village which men still call Tyre,
With leaden age o'ercargoed, dipping deep
For Famagusta and the hidden sun
That rings black Cyprus with a lake of fire;
And all those ships were certainly so old —
Who knows how oft with squat and noisy gun,
Questing brown slaves or Syrian oranges,
The pirate Genoese
Hell-raked them till they rolled
Blood, water, fruit and corpses up the hold?
But now through friendly seas they softly run,
Painted the mid-sea blue or shore-sea green,
Still patterned with the vine and grapes in gold.

But I have seen,
Pointing her shapely shadows from the dawn
An image tumbled on a rose-swept bay,
A drowsy ship of some yet older day;
And, wonder's breath indrawn,
Thought I — who knows — who knows but in that same
(Fished up beyond Aeaea, patched up new
— Stern painted brighter blue —)
That talkative bald-headed seaman came
(Twelve patient comrades sweating at the oar)
From Troy's doom-crimson shore,
And with great lies about his wooden horse
Set the crew laughing, and forgot his course?
It was so old a ship — who knows, who knows?
— And yet so beautiful, I watched in vain
To see the mast burst open with a rose,
And the whole deck put on its leaves again.

— *James Elroy Flecker*

THE LITTLE SHIPS

Who to the deeps in ships go down
   Great marvels do behold,
But comes the day when some must drown
   In the grey sea and cold.
For galleons lost great bells do toll,
   But now must we implore
God's ear for sunken Little Ships
   Who are not heard of more.

When ships of war put out to sea
   They go with guns and mail,
That so the chance may equal be
   Should foeman them assail;
But Little Ships men's errands run
   And are not clad for strife;
God's mercy then on Little Ships
   Who cannot fight for life.

To warm and cure, to clothe and feed
   They stoutly put to sea,
And since that men of them had need
   Made light of jeopardy;
Each in her hour her fate did meet
   Nor flinched nor made outcry;
God's love be with the Little Ships
   Who could not choose but die.

To friar and nun, and every one
   Who lives to save and tend,
Sisters were these whose work is done
   And cometh thus to end;

Full well they knew what risk they ran
  But still were strong to give;
God's grace for all the Little Ships
  Who died that men might live.

— Hilton Brown

'THEY THAT GO DOWN . . .'

They that go down to the sea in ships,
that do business in great waters;
these see the works of the Lord,
and his wonders in the deep.
For he commandeth, and raiseth the stormy wind,
which lifteth up the waves thereof.
They mount up to heaven,
they go down again to the depths:
their soul is melted because of trouble.
They reel to and fro, and stagger like a drunken man,
and are at their wits' end.
Then they cry unto the Lord in their trouble,
and he bringeth them out of their distresses.
He maketh the storm a calm,
so that the waves thereof are still;
Then they are glad because they be quiet;
so he bringeth them unto their desired haven.
Oh that men would praise the Lord for his goodness,
and for his wonderful works to the children of men!

— The Bible

Psalm **CVII:23-31**

197

MIRACLES

Why, who makes much of a miracle?
As to me I know of nothing else but miracles,
Whether I walk the streets of Manhattan,
Or dart my sight over the roofs of houses toward the sky,
Or wade with naked feet along the beach just in the edge
      of the water,
Or stand under trees in the woods,

  .   .   .   .

Or watch honey-bees busy around the hive of a summer
      forenoon,
Or animals feeding in the fields,
Or birds, or the wonderfulness of insects in the air,
Or the wonderfulness of the sundown, or of the stars
      shining so quiet and bright,
Or the exquisite delicate thin curve of the new moon in
      spring;
These with the rest, one and all, are to me miracles,
The whole referring, yet each distinct and in its place.

To me every hour of the light and dark is a miracle,
Every cubic inch of space is a miracle,
Every square yard of the surface of the earth is spread with
      the same,
Every foot of the interior swarms with the same.

To me the sea is a continual miracle,
The fishes that swim — the rocks — the motion of the waves
      — the ships with men in them,
What stranger miracles are there?

— Walt Whitman

THE SEED SHOP

Here in a quiet and dusty room they lie,
Faded as a crumbled stone or shifting sand,
Forlorn as ashes, shrivelled, scentless, dry —
Meadows and gardens running through my hand.

In this brown husk a dale of hawthorn dreams,
A cedar in this narrow cell is thrust;
It will drink deeply of a century's streams,
These lilies shall make summer on my dust.

Here in their safe and simple house of death,
Sealed in their shell a million roses leap;
Here I can blow a garden with my breath,
And in my hand a forest lies asleep.

— Muriel Stuart

'VIOLETS, DAFFODILS'

Violets, daffodils,
Roses and thorn
Were all in the garden
Before you were born.

Daffodils, violets,
Green thorn and roses
Your grandchildren's children
Will hold to their noses.

— Elizabeth Coatsworth

THE LILAC

Who thought of the lilac?
'I,' dew said,
'I made up the lilac
out of my head.'

'She made up the lilac!
Pooh!' thrilled a linnet,
and each dew-note had a
lilac in it.

— Humbert Wolfe

from: I STOOD TIP-TOE UPON A LITTLE HILL

Here are sweet peas, on tiptoe for a flight,
With wings of gentle flush o'er delicate white,
And taper fingers catching at all things,
To bind them all about with tiny rings.
Linger awhile upon some bending planks
That lean against a streamlet's rushy banks,
And watch intently Nature's gentle doings;
They will be found softer than a ring-dove's cooings.
How silent comes the water round the bend!
Not the minutest whisper does it send
To the o'erhanging sallows; blades of grass
Slowly across the checkered shadow pass.

— *John Keats*

SONG

The primrose in the green forest,
    The violets they be gay;
The double daisies, and the rest
That trimly decks the way,
Doth move the spirits with brave delights,
    Who Beauty's darlings be:

With hey tricksy, trim-go-tricksy,
    Under the greenwood tree.

— *Thomas Deloney*

from: THE LEGEND OF GOOD WOMEN

... of all the flowers in the mead,
Then love I most these flowers white and red
Such as men callen daisies in our town.
To them I have so great affection,
As I said first, when comen is the May,
That in my bed there dawneth me no day,
That I am (not) up, and walking in the mead,
To see this flower in the sunshine spread,
When it upriseth early in the morrow,
That blissful sight soft'neth all my sorrow.
　　And when that it is eve, I blithely run,
As soon as ever the sun goeth west,
To see this flower, how it will go to rest,
For fear of night, so hateth she darkness! ...

— *Geoffrey Chaucer*

'WHAT A DAINTY LIFE ...'

What a dainty life the milkmaid leads,
When over the flowery meads
She dabbles in the dew
And sings to her cow,
And feels not the pain
Of love or disdain!
She sleeps in the night, though she toils in the day,
And merrily passeth her time away.

— *Thomas Nabbes*

𝄞 DABBLING IN THE DEW

Oh, where are you going to, my pretty little dear,
With your red rosy cheeks and your coal-black hair?
I'm going a-milking, kind sir, she answered me:
And it's dabbling in the dew makes the milkmaids fair!

Suppose I were to clothe you, my pretty little dear,
In a green silken gown and the amethyst so rare?
O no, sir, O no, sir, kind sir, she answered me,
For it's dabbling in the dew makes the milkmaids fair.

Suppose I were to carry you, my pretty little dear,
In a chariot with horses, a grey gallant pair?
O no, sir, O no, sir, kind sir, she answered me,
For it's dabbling in the dew makes the milkmaids fair.

Suppose I were to feast you, my pretty little dear,
With dainties on silver, the whole of the year?
O no, sir, O no, sir, kind sir, she answered me,
For it's dabbling in the dew makes the milkmaids fair.

O but London's a city, my pretty little dear,
And all men are gallant and brave that are there —
O no, sir, O no, sir, kind sir, she answered me,
For it's dabbling in the dew makes the milkmaids fair.

O fine clothes and dainties and carriages so rare,
Bring grey to the cheeks and silver to the hair;
What's a ring on the finger if rings are round the eye?
But it's dabbling in the dew makes the milkmaids fair!

— Traditional: English

♪ THE MILK-MAID

'Where be ye goin', sweet little maiden,
  Where be ye goin' in the mornin'?
Where be ye goin', cheeks so rosy reddin'
  Early, so early in the mornin'?

'Where be ye goin', sweet little maiden,
  Where be ye goin' in the mornin'?
Hair is so blacken as the wing of a raven,
  Early, so early in the mornin'.'

'I be a-milkin', milkin' for my father,
  And for my mother in the mornin';
I be a milkin' for my little sister,
  Early, so early in the mornin'.'

'How come ye fair so early in the mornin'
  How come ye fair, sweet little maiden?'
'Charm have I none, nor thought of beauty given,
  Save for my dew-dabblin' in the mornin'.'

'Say will you wed me, sweet little maiden,
  Wed me so early in the mornin',
Lady I'll make thee, house and lands bring to thee,
  Say will you wed me in the mornin'?'

'Have you a cow, sir, that milkin' needs, sir,
  Milkin' so early in the mornin'?
Then I'll agree, sir, marry thee with glee, sir, and,
  Do my dew-dabblin' in the mornin'.'

— Traditional: American

206

♪ 'O MISTRESS MINE...'

O mistress mine, where are you roaming?
O, stay and hear — your true love's coming,
   That can sing both high and low:
Trip no further, pretty sweeting;
Journeys end in lovers' meeting,
   Every wise man's son doth know.

What is love? 'tis not hereafter;
Present mirth hath present laughter;
   What's to come is still unsure:
In delay there lies no plenty:
Then come kiss me, sweet-and-twenty!
   Youth's a stuff will not endure.

— *William Shakespeare*

from: *Twelfth Night,* Act II, Scene 3

♪ I KNOW WHERE I'M GOING

I know where I'm going,
I know who's going with me,
I know who I love,
But the dear knows who I'll marry.

I'll have stockings of silk,
Shoes of fine green leather,
Combs to buckle my hair
And a ring for every finger.

Feather beds are soft,
Painted rooms are bonny;
But I'd leave them all
To go with my love Johnny.

Some say he's dark,
I say he's bonny,
He's the flower of them all,
My handsome, coaxing Johnny.

I know where I'm going,
I know who's going with me,
I know who I love,
But the dear knows who I'll marry.

— Modern Irish, author unknown

THE PASSIONATE SHEPHERD TO HIS LOVE

Come live with me, and be my love,
And we will all the pleasures prove
That hills and valleys, dales and fields,
And all the craggy mountains yields.

And we will sit upon the rocks,
Seeing the shepherds feed their flocks
By shallow rivers, to whose falls
Melodious birds sing madrigals.

And I will make thee beds of roses,
And a thousand fragrant posies,
A cap of flowers and a kirtle
Embroider'd all with leaves of myrtle.

A gown made of the finest wool
Which from our pretty lambs we pull,
Fair lined slippers for the cold,
With buckles of the purest gold.

A belt of straw and ivy-buds,
With coral clasps and amber studs,
And if these pleasures may thee move,
Come live with me, and be my love.

Thy silver dishes for thy meat,
As precious as the gods do eat,
Shall on an ivory table be
Prepar'd each day for thee and me.

The shepherd swains shall dance and sing
For thy delight each May-morning;
If these delights thy mind may move,
Then live with me, and be my love.

— *Christopher Marlowe*

𝄞 THE KEYS OF CANTERBURY

O Madam, I will give to you
The keys of Canterbury,
And all the bells in London
Shall ring to make us merry,
If you will be my joy, my sweet and only dear,
And walk along with me, anywhere.

I shall not, Sir, accept of you
The keys of Canterbury,
Nor all the bells in London
Shall ring to make us merry,
I will not be your joy, your sweet and only dear,
Nor walk along with you, anywhere.

O Madam, I will give to you
A pair of boots of cork;
The one was made in London,
The other made in York,
If you will be my joy, my sweet and only dear,
And walk along with me, anywhere.

I shall not, Sir, accept of you
A pair of boots of cork,
Though both were made in London,
Or both were made in York.
I will not be your joy, your sweet and only dear,
Nor walk along with you, anywhere.

O Madam, I will give to you
A little golden bell,
To ring for all your servants
And make them serve you well,
If you will be my joy, my sweet and only dear,
And walk along with me, anywhere.

I shall not, Sir, accept of you
A little golden bell,
To ring for all my servants
To make them serve me well;
I will not be your joy, your sweet and only dear,
Nor walk along with you, anywhere.

O Madam, I will give to you
A gallant silver chest,
With a key of gold and silver,
And jewels of the best,
If you will be my joy, my sweet and only dear,
And walk along with me, anywhere.

I shall not, Sir, accept of you
A gallant silver chest,
A key of gold and silver
Nor jewels of the best.
I will not be your joy, your sweet and only dear,
Nor walk along with you, anywhere.

O Madam, I will give to you
A broidered silken gownd,
With nine yards a-drooping
And training on the ground,
If you will be my joy, my sweet and only dear,
And walk along with me, anywhere.

O Sir, I will accept of you
A broidered silken gownd,
With nine yards a-drooping
And training on the ground:
Then I will be your joy, your sweet and only dear,
And walk along with you, anywhere.

— Traditional: English

THE FORTUNE SEEKER

Hollyhocks slant in the wind,
Gallantly blowing,
Crinkled and purfled and lined,
Thank God for their growing.
Their burden is only of bees,
Banded and brown,
But she, O, she's
The worth of my world on her head for a crown.
How can she step it so freely, so lightly,
Her head like a star on a stem showing whitely,
How can she carry her
Wealth with that innocent air?
I'm going to marry her, marry her, marry her,
Just for the wealth of her hair.

Larkspurs as deep as a pool,
Lilies like ladies,
Silvered and silked where the cool
Elder tree shade is,
These are the queens of the sun,
Splendid and sweet,
But she, my one
Flower's without price from her head to her feet.

How can she go by the lanes and the ditches,
Her little proud head unbowed by its riches?
How can she carry her
Fortune so light in the air?
I'm going to marry her, marry her, marry her,
Just for the wealth of her hair.

— *Marjorie Pickthall*

purfled: bordered, edged.

'I WILL MAKE YOU BROOCHES . . .'

I will make you brooches and toys for your delight
Of bird-song at morning and star-shine at night.
I will make a palace fit for you and me
Of green days in forests and blue days at sea.

I will make my kitchen, and you shall keep your room,
Where white flows the river and bright blows the broom,
And you shall wash your linen and keep your body white
In rainfall at morning and dewfall at night.

And this shall be for music when no one else is near,
The fine song for singing, the rare song to hear!
That only I remember, that only you admire,
Of the broad road that stretches and the roadside fire.

— Robert Louis Stevenson

AEDH WISHES FOR THE CLOTHS OF HEAVEN

Had I the heavens' embroidered cloths,
Enwrought with gold and silver light,
The blue and the dim and the dark cloths
Of night and light and the half-light,
I would spread the cloths under your feet:
But I, being poor, have only my dreams;
I have spread my dreams under your feet;
Tread softly because you tread on my dreams.

— William Butler Yeats

SUNRISE AND SUNSET

I'll tell you how the sun rose, —
A ribbon at a time.
The steeples swam in amethyst,
The news like squirrels ran.

The hills untied their bonnets,
The bobolinks begun.
Then I said softly to myself,
'That must have been the sun!'

But how he set, I know not.
There seemed a purple stile
Which little yellow boys and girls
Were climbing all the while

Till when they reached the other side,
A dominie in gray
Put gently up the evening bars,
And led the flock away.

— *Emily Dickinson*

THE WEATHER

A red sky at night is the shepherd's delight;
A red sky at morning is the shepherd's warning.

———————

Evening red and morning gray
Send the sailor on his way;
Evening gray and morning red
Bring down rains upon his head.

———————

Evening red and morning gray,
It is the sign of a bonny day;
Evening gray and morning red,
The lamb and ewe go wet to bed.

———————

When the wind is in the east,
'Tis neither good for man nor beast;

When the wind is in the north
The skilful fisher goes not forth;

When the wind is in the south
It blows the bait in the fishes' mouth;

When the wind is in the west,
Then 'tis at the very best.

———————

When the clouds of the morn
To the west fly away,
You may depend
On a fair settled day.

———————

217

When clouds appear
Like rocks and towers,
The earth's refreshed
By frequent showers.

— *Traditional: English and Scots*

THE MONTHS

January cold desolate;
February dripping wet;
March wind ranges;
April changes;
Birds sing in tune
To flowers of May,
And sunny June
Brings longest day;
In scorched July
The storm-clouds fly,
Lightning-torn;
August bears corn,
September fruit;
In rough October
Earth must disrobe her;
Stars fall and shoot
In keen November;
And night is long
And cold is strong
In bleak December.

— *Christina Rossetti*

A JANUARY MORNING

The glittering roofs are still with frost; each worn
Black chimney builds into the quiet sky
Its curling pile to crumble silently.
Far out to the westward on the edge of morn,
The slender misty city towers up-borne
Glimmer faint rose against the pallid blue;
And yonder, on those northern hills, the hue
Of amethyst, hang fleeces dull as horn.

And here behind me come the woodmen's sleighs
With shouts and clamorous squeakings; might and
    main
Up the steep slope the horses stamp and strain,
Urged on by hoarse-tongued drivers — cheeks ablaze,
Iced beards and frozen eyelids — team by team,
With frost-fringed flanks, and nostrils jetting steam.

— Archibald Lampman

WINTER

In rigorous hours, when down the iron lane
The redbreast looks in vain
For hips and haws,
Lo, shining flowers upon my window-pane
The silver pencil of the winter draws.

When all the snowy hill
And the bare woods are still;
When snipes are silent in the frozen bogs,
And all the garden garth is whelmed in mire,
Lo, by the hearth, the laughter of the logs —
More fair than roses, lo, the flowers of fire!

— *Robert Louis Stevenson*

THE SNOWFLAKE

Before I melt,
Come, look at me!
This lovely icy filigree!
Of a great forest
In one night
I make a wilderness
Of white:
By skyey cold
Of crystals made,
All softly, on
Your finger laid,
I pause, that you
My beauty see:
Breathe, and I vanish
Instantly.

— *Walter de la Mare*

TO A SNOWFLAKE

What heart could have thought you? —
Past our devisal
(O filigree petal!)
Fashioned so purely,
Fragilely, surely,
From what Paradisal
Imagineless metal,
Too costly for cost?
Who hammered you, wrought you,
From argentine vapour?
'God was my shaper.
Passing surmisal,
He hammered, He wrought me,
From curled silver vapour,
To lust of his mind: —
Thou couldst not have thought me!
So purely, so palely,
Tinily, surely,
Mightily, frailly,
Insculped and embossed,
With His hammer of wind,
And His graver of frost.'

— *Francis Thompson*

LONDON SNOW

When men were all asleep the snow came flying,
In large white flakes falling on the city brown,
Stealthily and perpetually settling and loosely lying,
   Hushing the latest traffic of the drowsy town;
Deadening, muffling, stifling its murmurs failing;
Lazily and incessantly floating down and down:
   Silently sifting and veiling road, roof and railing;
Hiding difference, making unevenness even,
Into angles and crevices softly drifting and sailing;
   All night it fell, and when full inches seven
It lay in the depth of its uncompacted lightness,
The clouds blew off from a high and frosty heaven;
   And all woke earlier for the unaccustomed brightness
Of the winter dawning, the strange unheavenly glare:
The eye marvelled — marvelled at the dazzling whiteness;
   The ear hearkened to the stillness of the solemn air;
No sound of wheel rumbling nor of foot falling,
And the busy morning cries came thin and spare.
   Then boys I heard, as they went to school, calling,
They gathered up the crystal manna to freeze
Their tongues with tasting, their hands with snowballing;
   Or rioted in a drift, plunging up to the knees;
Or peering up from under the white-mossed wonder,
'O look at the trees!' they cried, 'O look at the trees!'
   With lessened load a few carts creak and blunder,
Following along the white deserted way,
A country company long dispersed asunder:
   When now already the sun, in pale display
Standing by Paul's high dome, spread forth below
His sparkling beams, and awoke the stir of the day.
   For now doors open, and war is waged with the snow;

And trains of sombre men, past tale of number,
Tread long brown paths, as toward their toil they go:
  But even for them awhile no cares encumber
Their minds diverted; the daily word is unspoken,
The daily thoughts of labour and sorrow slumber
At the sight of the beauty that greets them, for the charm
    they have broken.

— Robert Bridges

WHITE FIELDS

I

In the winter time we go
Walking in the fields of snow;

Where there is no grass at all;
Where the top of every wall,

Every fence and every tree,
Is as white as white can be.

II

Pointing out the way we came,
— Every one of them the same —

All across the fields there be
Prints in silver filigree;

And our mothers always know,
By the footprints in the snow,

Where it is the children go.

— James Stephens

THE FIR TREES TAPER INTO TWIGS

The fir trees taper into twigs and wear
The rich blue green of summer all the year,
Softening the roughest tempest almost calm
And offering shelter still and warm
To the small path that towels underneath,
Where loudest winds — almost as summer's breath —
Scarce fans the weed that lingers green below,
When others out of doors are lost in frost and snow.
And sweet the music trembles on the ear
As the wind suthers through each tiny spear,
Makeshifts for leaves; and yet, so rich they show,
Winter is almost summer where they grow.

— John Clare

IN FEBRUARY

Now in the dark of February rains,
    Poor lovers of the sunshine, spring is born,
    The earthy fields are full of hidden corn,
And March's violets bud along the lanes;

Therefore with joy believe in what remains.
    And thou who dost not feel them, do not scorn
    Our early songs for winter overworn,
And faith in God's handwriting on the plains.

'Hope,' writes he, 'Love' in the first violet,
'Joy,' even from Heaven, in songs and winds and trees;
And having caught the happy words in these
While Nature labours with the letters yet,
Spring cannot cheat us, though her hopes be broken,
Nor leave us, for we know what God hath spoken.

— *George Macdonald*

SPRING QUIET

Gone were but the winter,
   Come were but the spring,
I would go to a covert
   Where the birds sing;

Where in the whitethorn
   Singeth the thrush,
And a robin sings
   In the holly-bush.

Full of fresh scents
   Are the budding boughs
Arching high over
   A cool green house;

Full of sweet scents,
   And whispering air
Which sayeth softly:
   'We spread no snare;

'Here dwell in safety,
   Here dwell alone,
With a clear stream
   And a mossy stone.

'Here the sun shineth
   Most shadily;
Here is heard an echo
   Of the far sea,
     Though far off it be.'

— Christina Rossetti

WINTER'S END

Outside the window, dark and still,
Lambs are calling upon the hill
With a bleating, wavering, quavering cry,
Calling and calling, they don't know why.
They are so little, so leggy, so lost,
They hate the dark and they fear the frost;
All of them running, sisters and brothers,
Calling aloud for their milky mothers.
None of them guesses, how could they know,
That a warm wind out of the south will blow
To soften the grass with sun and showers,
To waken the birds and shake the flowers,
To bring the babies out of their wraps,
Their gaiters and woollies, their mittens and caps,
All the babies, so round and sweet,
Waving their hands and their dimpled feet
To welcome the light and the kind spring weather
When lambs and children can play together.

— *Eiluned Lewis*

'... THE WINTER IS PAST'

For lo, the winter is past,
the rain is over and gone,
the flowers appear on the earth;
the time of the singing of birds is come,
and the voice of the turtle is heard in our land.

— *The Bible*

The Song of Solomon II:11-12

WINTER IN MARCH

While Resting on the Bridge at the Foot of Brother's Water

The cock is crowing,
The stream is flowing,
The small birds twitter,
The lake doth glitter,
The green field sleeps in the sun;
The oldest and youngest
Are at work with the strongest;
The cattle are grazing,
Their heads never raising;
There are forty feeding like one!

Like an army defeated
The snow hath retreated,
And now doth fare ill
On the top of the bare hill;
The plowboy is whooping — anon — anon:
There's joy in the mountains;
There's life in the fountains;
Small clouds are sailing,
Blue sky prevailing;
The rain is over and gone!

— William Wordsworth

APRIL SHOWERS

The leaves are fresh after the rain,
The air is cool and clear,
The sun is shining warm again,
The sparrows hopping in the lane
Are brisk and full of cheer.

And that is why we dance and play,
And that is why we sing,
Calling out in voices gay,
We will not go to school today
Nor learn anything!

It is a happy thing, I say,
To be alive on such a day.

— James Stephens

♪ SPRING

Sound the flute!
Now it's mute.
Birds delight
Day and Night;
Nightingale
In the dale,
Lark in Sky,
Merrily,
Merrily, merrily, to welcome in the Year.

Little Boy,
Full of joy;
Little Girl,
Sweet and small;
Cock does crow,
So do you;
Merry voice,
Infant noise,
Merrily, merrily, to welcome in the Year.

Little Lamb,
Here I am;
Come and lick
My white neck;
Let me pull
Your soft Wool;
Let me kiss
Your soft face;
Merrily, merrily, we welcome in the Year.

— *William Blake*

♪ EASTER

I got me flowers to straw thy way,
I got me boughs off many a tree;
But thou wast up by break of day,
And brought'st thy sweets along with thee.

The Sun arising in the East,
Though he give light, and the East perfume,
If they should offer to contest
With thy arising, they presume.

Can there be any day but this,
Though many suns to shine endeavour?
We count three hundred, but we miss:
There is but one, and that one ever.

— George Herbert

A PAGE'S ROAD SONG

(Thirteenth Century)

Jesu,
   If thou wilt make
Thy peach trees bloom for me,
And fringe my bridle path both sides
   With tulips, red and free,
If Thou wilt make Thy skies as blue
   As ours in Sicily,
And wake the little leaves that sleep
   On every bending tree —
I promise not to vexen Thee

That Thou shouldst make eternally
   Heaven my home;
But right contentedly,
A singing page I'll be
   Here in Thy springtime,
   Jesu.

— William Alexander Percy

'LOVELIEST OF TREES . . .'

Loveliest of trees, the cherry now
Is hung with bloom along the bough,
And stands about the woodland ride
Wearing white for Eastertide.

Now, of my threescore years and ten,
Twenty will not come again,
And take from seventy springs a score,
It only leaves me fifty more.

And since to look at things in bloom
Fifty springs are little room,
About the woodlands I will go
To see the cherry hung with snow.

— A. E. Housman

♪ THE MAYERS' SONG

We've been a-rambling all this night,
And sometime of this day;
And now returning back again
We bring a branch of May.

A branch of May we bring you here,
And at your door it stands;
It is but a sprout well budded out,
The work of Our Lord's hands.

The hedges and trees they are so green,
As green as any leek;
Our heavenly Father, He watered them
With His heavenly dew so sweet.

The heavenly gates are open wide,
Our paths are beaten plain;
And if a man be not too far gone,
He may return again.

So dear, so dear as Christ loved us,
And for our sins was slain,
Christ bids us turn from wickedness
Back to the Lord again.

The moon shines bright, the stars give a light
A little before it is day,
So God bless you all, both great and small,
And send you a joyful May.

— Traditional: English

AS WE DANCE ROUND A-RING-A-RING

As we dance round a-ring-a-ring,
A maiden goes a-maying;
And here a flower, and there a flower,
Through mead and meadow straying:
O gentle one, why dost thou weep?
Silver to spend with; gold to keep;
Till spin the green round World asleep,
And Heaven its dews be staying.

— *Anonymous*

♪ ON MAY MORNING

Now the bright morning Star, Daye's harbinger,
Comes dancing from the East, and leads with her
The Flowery May, who from her green lap throws
The yellow Cowslip, and the pale Primrose.
　　Hail, bounteous May! that dost inspire
　　Mirth, and youth, and warm desire;
　　Woods and Groves are of thy dressing;
　　Hill and Dale doth boast thy blessing.
Thus we salute thee with our early Song,
And welcome thee, and wish thee long.

— *John Milton*

THE CHERRY TREE

Come from your bed, my drowsy gentleman!
And you, fair lady, rise and braid your hair!
And bid the children wash, if that they can;
If not, assist you them, and make them fair
As is the morning, and the morning sky,
And all the sun doth warm in golden air.

For he has climbed the height these times ago!
He laughed about the hills and they were glad;
With bubbled pearl he set the stream aglow
And laced the hedge in silver; and he clad
The lawn in pomp of green, and white, and gold;
And bade the world forget it had been sad.

Then lift yourself, good sir! And you, sweet dame,
Unlash your evening eyes of pious grey!
Call on the children by each lovéd name,
And set them on the grass and bid them play;
And play with them awhile, and sing with them,
Beneath the cherry bush, a rondelay.

— *James Stephens*

TO AN ORCHARD NEAR LONDON

('This Land to be Sold in Building Plots')

Bloom passionately, O apple-trees, this spring;
Drink deep of the April sun, the April rain,
That this may be your loveliest blossoming,
O apple-trees that shall not flower again.

And let your apples rounder and sweeter grow
   This year than they have ever grown before;
Under their burden let your boughs bend low —
   When these are gathered you shall bear no more.

Bloom passionately, then, this last long spring,
That to the very air your ghost may cling
In after years when roofs and walls shine red
Where once your rosy apples shone instead;
And where your topmost boughs once caught the breeze
Some child may sleep — and dream of apple-trees.

— Jan Struther

from: CHORIC SONG

There is sweet music here that softer falls
Than petals from blown roses on the grass,
Or night-dews on still waters between walls
Of shadowy granite, in a gleaming pass;
Music that gentlier on the spirit lies,
Than tired eyelids upon tired eyes;
Music that brings sweet sleep down from the blissful skies.
Here are cool mosses deep,
And thro' the moss the ivies creep,
And in the stream the long-leaved flowers weep,
And from the craggy ledge the poppy hangs in sleep.

— Alfred, Lord Tennyson

from: *The Lotos-Eaters*

♪ A GREAT TIME

Sweet Chance, that led my steps abroad,
　　Beyond the town, where wild flowers grow —
A rainbow and a cuckoo, Lord,
　　How rich and great the times are now!
　　　　Know, all ye sheep
　　　　And cows, that keep
On staring that I stand so long
　　In grass that's wet from heavy rain —
A rainbow and a cuckoo's song
　　May never come together again;
　　　　May never come
　　　　This side the tomb.

— W. H. Davies

A SOFT DAY

　　A soft day, thank God!
　　A wind from the south
　　With a honeyed mouth;
　　A scent of drenching leaves,
　　Briar and beech and lime,
　　White elder-flower and thyme,

And the soaking grass smells sweet,
Crushed by my two bare feet,
　　While the rain drips,
Drips, drips, drips from the leaves.

　　A soft day, thank God!
　　The hills wear a shroud
　　Of silver cloud;

The web the spider weaves
Is a glittering net;
The woodland path is wet,

And the soaking earth smells sweet,
Under my two bare feet,
    And the rain drips,
Drips, drips, drips from the leaves.

— Winifred M. Letts

♫ WEATHERS

This is the weather the cuckoo likes,
        And so do I;
When showers betumble the chestnut spikes,
        And nestlings fly:
And the little brown nightingale bills his best,
And they sit outside at 'The Travellers' Rest,'
And maids come forth sprig-muslin drest,
And citizens dream of the south and west,
        And so do I.

This is the weather the shepherd shuns,
        And so do I;
When beeches drip in browns and duns,
        And thresh, and ply;
And hill-hid tides throb, throe on throe,
And meadow rivulets overflow,
And drops on gate-bars hang in a row,
And rooks in families homeward go,
        And so do I.

— Thomas Hardy

239

THE RAINY SUMMER

There's much afoot in heaven and earth this year;
  The winds hunt up the sun, hunt up the moon,
Trouble the dubious dawn, hasten the drear
  Height of a threatening noon.

No breath of boughs, no breath of leaves, of fronds,
  May linger or grow warm; the trees are loud;
The forest, rooted, tosses in her bonds,
  And strains against the cloud.

No scents may pause within the garden-fold;
  The rifled flowers are cold as ocean-shells;
Bees, humming in the storm, carry their cold
  Wild honey to cold cells.

— Alice Meynell

WORLDS

Through the pale green forest of tall bracken-stalks,
Whose interwoven fronds, a jade-green sky,
Above me glimmer, infinitely high,
Toward my giant hand a beetle walks
In glistening emerald mail; and as I lie
Watching his progress through huge grassy blades
And over pebble boulders, my own world fades
And shrinks to the vision of a beetle's eye.

Within that forest world of twilight green
Ambushed with unknown perils, one endless day
I travel down the beetle-trail between

Huge glossy boles through green infinity . . .
Till flashes a glimpse of the blue sea through the bracken
      asway,
And my world is again a tumult of windy sea.

— W. W. Gibson

HILL PASTURES

High on the hill the curlews and the whimbrels
Go mating all day long with a sweet whistle;
With a sound of chiming bells and shaken timbrels,
And silver rings that fall in a crystal cup.
They laugh, as lovers laugh when the moon is up,
Over the cotton grass and the carline-thistle.

Poised in his airy spiral the snipe is calling,
Summoning love with a music mournful and lonely
As a lost lamb in the night, rising, falling,
Stranger than any melody, wilder than song.
He cries of life that is short, and death that is long,
Telling his dusky love to one heart only.

Once in seven days a plaintive ringing
Sounds from the little chapel high in the heather,
Out with the sorrowful snipe and the whimbrel winging.
The wild hill ponies hear it there as they graze,
And whinny, and call to their foals, and stand at gaze,
Hearing a clear voice in the clear weather.

And out of pine-dark farms and windy places,
And quiet cottages low in the valley hiding,
Brown folk come with still and wistful faces.

241

Straying by twos and threes, like the peaceful sheep,
Into the small brown shippen of souls they creep,
Seeking a calm like the hills', but more abiding.

— Mary Webb

from: THE SUN'S DARLING

Haymakers, rakers, reapers, and mowers,
  Wait on your summer queen.
Dress up with musk-rose her eglantine bowers,
  Daffodils strew the green.
    Sing, dance and play,
    'Tis holiday.
The sun doth bravely shine
On our ears of corn.
    Rich as a pearl,
    Comes every girl,
This is mine, this is mine, this is mine;
Let us die, ere away they be borne.

Bow to the sun, to our queen, and that fair one,
  Come to behold our sports.
Each bonny lass here is counted a rare one,
  As those in princes' courts.
    These and we
    With country glee,
Will teach the woods to resound
And the hills with echoes hollow;
    Skipping lambs
    Their bleating dams
'Mongst kids shall trip it round;
For joy thus our wenches we follow.

242

Wind, jolly huntsmen, your neat bugles shrilly,
　　Hounds make a lusty cry;
Spring up, you falconers, the partridges freely,
　　Then let your brave hawks fly.
　　　　Horses amain
　　　　Over ridge, over plain,
　　The dogs have the stag in chase;
　　'Tis a sport to content a king:
　　　　So, ho! ho! through the skies
　　　　How the proud bird flies,
　　And sousing, kills with a grace.
Now the deer falls; hark! how they ring.

　　　　　　　　　　　　— *Thomas Dekker*

LABOR OF FIELDS

July is honored with the labor of fields
That round against the sky in standing grain,
So beautiful the breath comes quick to see them.
It is the month men pray for little rain
So they may cut their hay and spread it out
Tossing it over for the sun to dry
And bring it safely to the empty barns
Before the clouds have massed too dark and high.

It is the month of sweat and weariness,
Of the arm aching with the scythe's slow weight,
Of horses straining heavily up the road
Through lengthening shadows as the hour grows late.
In river lowlands, ledged fields by the sea,
And sloping inland valleys far away
The old laborious ritual is performed —
Once more, once more men gather in the hay.

— Elizabeth Coatsworth

THE TUFT OF FLOWERS

I went to turn the grass once after one
Who mowed it in the dew before the sun.

The dew was gone that made his blade so keen
Before I came to view the levelled scene.

I looked for him behind an isle of trees;
I listened for his whetstone on the breeze.

But he had gone his way, the grass all mown,
And I must be, as he had been — alone,

'As all must be,' I said within my heart,
'Whether they work together or apart.'

But as I said it, swift there passed me by
On noiseless wing a bewildered butterfly,

Seeking with memories grown dim o'er night
Some resting flower of yesterday's delight.

And once I marked his flight go round and round,
As where some flower lay withering on the ground.

And then he flew as far as eye could see,
And then on tremulous wing came back to me.

I thought of questions that have no reply,
And would have turned to toss the grass to dry;

But he turned first, and led my eye to look
At a tall tuft of flowers beside a brook,

A leaping tongue of bloom the scythe had spared
Beside a reedy brook the scythe had bared.

I left my place to know them by their name,
Finding them butterfly weed when I came.

The mower in the dew had loved them thus,
By leaving them to flourish, not for us,

Nor yet to draw one thought of ours to him.
But from sheer morning gladness at the brim.

The butterfly and I had lit upon,
Nevertheless a message from the dawn,

That made me hear the wakening birds around,
And hear his long scythe whispering to the ground,

And feel a spirit kindred to my own;
So that henceforth I worked no more alone;

But glad with him, I worked as with his aid,
And weary, sought at noon with him the shade;

And dreaming, as it were, held brotherly speech
With one whose thought I had not hoped to reach.

'Men work together,' I told him from the heart,
'Whether they work together or apart.'

— Robert Frost

HAY HARVEST

I met a man mowing
  A meadow of hay;
So smoothly and flowing
  His swathes fell away,
    At break of the day
    Up Hambledon way;
A yellow-eyed collie
  Was guarding his coat —
Loose-limbed and lob-lolly,
  But wise and remote;

The morning came leaping, —
  'Twas five o' the clock,
The world was still sleeping
  At Hambledon Lock, —
    As sound as a rock
    Slept village and Lock;
'Fine morning!' the man says,
  And I says, 'Fine day!'
Then I to my fancies
  And he to his hay!

And lovely and quiet,
  And lonely and chill,
Lay river and eyot,
  And meadow and mill; —
    I think of them still —
    Mead, river and mill;
For wasn't it jolly
  With only us three —
The yellow-eyed collie,
  The mower and me?

            — *Patrick R. Chalmers*

eyot: a small river island with willows growing on it.

THE SALT HAY

This is the hay that no man planted,
This is the ground that was never plowed,
Watered by tides, cold and brackish,
Shadowed by fog and the sea-born cloud.

This is the crop above which sounded
No bobolink's song, but the gull's long cry,
That men now reap as they reap their meadows
And mound in the great gold stacks to dry.

In the long winter months when deep pile the snowdrifts
And the cattle stand in the dusk all day
Many a cow shall taste pale seaweed
Twined in the stalks of the wild salt hay.

— Elizabeth Coatsworth

I WILL GO WITH MY FATHER A-PLOUGHING

I will go with my Father a-ploughing
To the Green Field by the sea,
And the rooks and corbies and seagulls
Will come flocking after me.
I will sing to the patient horses
With the lark in the shine of the air,
And my Father will sing the Plough-Song
That blesses the cleaving share.

I will go with my Father a-sowing
To the Red Field by the sea,
And the merls and robins and thrushes
Will come flocking after me.
I will sing to the striding sowers
With the finch on the flowering sloe,
And my Father will sing the Seed-Song
That only the wise men know.

I will go with my Father a-reaping
To the Brown Field by the sea,
And the geese and pigeons and sparrows
Will come flocking after me.
I will sing to the weary reapers
With the wren in the heat of the sun,
And my Father will sing the Scythe-Song
That joys for the harvest done.

— *Joseph Campbell*

HYMN FOR HARVEST-TIDE

Now beautifully barley, wheat and oats
   Glister in harvest cloth-of-gold ashine,
And round the fields with musical glad throats   ˏ
   Birds of the Autumn hymn Thy care divine,
         Most bounteous Lord;
         And we take up the word
     Of glory to the Giver of all good things,
         And each heart sings.

Full with ripe plenty, every meadow's breast
   Breathes of Thine opulent promise all fulfilled,
Sweet plains in yellow and red and silver drest
   To noble praise their loveliness do yield,
         And we take up this word,
         Most bounteous Lord,
     Of glory to the Giver of all good things,
         And each heart sings.

While wind and light weave gentlest symphony
   Floating athwart the radiant swaying corn,
And nimble amber brooks add melody
   Of mirthful descant bird-songs to adorn,
         We raise anew our word,
         Most bounteous Lord,
     Of glory to the Giver of all good things,
         And each heart sings.

For increase and full harvest and safe store
   Of provender whereof Thou fashionest all,
We, with all things created, less and more,
   Thy care benign adore in festival,

Most bounteous Lord,
Yea, we renew that word
Of glory to the Giver of all good things,
And each heart sings.

Hearts glad to be alive and thankful minds
And quiet fancy bring we, and rejoice
In fruit of field, of love and pain, that finds —
After long patience — benediction's voice.
Most bounteous Lord,
To Thee we raise this word
Of glory to the Giver of all good things,
And each heart sings.

— *W. H. Hamilton*

GOD'S WORLD

O World, I cannot hold thee close enough!
Thy winds, thy wide grey skies!
Thy mists, that roll and rise!
Thy woods, this autumn day, that ache and sag
And all but cry with color! That gaunt crag
To crush! To lift the lean of that black bluff!
World, World, I cannot get thee close enough!

Long have I known a glory in it all,
But never knew I this;
Here such a passion is
As stretcheth me apart, — Lord, I do fear
Thou'st made the world too beautiful this year;
My soul is all but out of me, — let fall
No burning leaf; prithee, let no bird call.

— *Edna St. Vincent Millay*

SONG

The feathers of the willow
Are half of them grown yellow
  Above the swelling stream;
And ragged are the bushes,
And rusty are the rushes
  And wild the clouded gleam.

The thistle now is older,
His stalk begins to moulder,
  His head is white as snow;
The branches all are barer,
The linnet's song is rarer
  The robin pipeth now.

— Richard Watson Dixon

from: AUTUMN

I saw old Autumn in the misty morn
Stand shadowless like Silence, listening
To silence, for no lonely bird would sing
Into his hollow ear from woods forlorn,
Nor lowly hedge nor solitary thorn;
Shaking his languid locks all dewy bright
With tangled gossamer that fell by night,
  Pearling his coronet of golden corn.

.   .   .   .

The squirrel gloats on his accomplished hoard,
The ants have brimmed their garners with ripe grain,
    And honey bees have stored
The sweets of Summer in their luscious cells;
The swallows all have winged across the main.

   •   •   •   •   •   •   •   •   •

— Thomas Hood

DIGGING

Today I think
Only with scents, — scents dead leaves yield,
And bracken, and wild carrot's seed,
And the square mustard field;

Odours that rise
When the spade wounds the root of tree,
Rose, currant, raspberry, or goutweed,
Rhubarb or celery;

The smoke's smell, too,
Flowing from where a bonfire burns
The dead, the waste, the dangerous,
And all to sweetness turns.

It is enough
To smell, to crumble the dark earth,
While the robin sings over again
Sad songs of Autumn mirth.

— Edward Thomas

GATHERING LEAVES

Spades take up leaves
No better than spoons,
And bags full of leaves
Are light as balloons.

I make a great noise
Of rustling all day
Like rabbit and deer
Running away.

But the mountains I move
Elude my embrace,
Flowing over my arms
And into my face.

I may load and unload
Again and again
Till I fill the whole shed,
And what have I then?

Next to nothing for weight,
And since they grew duller
From contact with earth,
Next to nothing for color.

Next to nothing for use.
But a crop is a crop,
And who's to say where
The harvest shall stop?

— *Robert Frost*

THE LAST WORD OF A BLUEBIRD

As I went out, a Crow
In a low voice said 'Oh,
I was looking for you
To tell Lesley (will you?)
That her little Bluebird
Wanted me to bring word
That the north wind last night,
That made the stars bright
And made ice on the trough,
Almost made him cough
His tail feathers off.
He just had to fly!
But he sent her Good-bye
And said to be good,
And wear her red hood,
And look for skunk tracks
In the snow with an axe —
And do everything!
And perhaps in the spring
He would come back and sing.'

— *Robert Frost*

LATE OCTOBER

I found ten kinds of wild flowers growing
On a steely day that looked like snowing;
Queen Anne's lace, and blue heal-all,
A buttercup, straggling, grown so tall,
A rusty aster, a chicory flower —
Ten I found in half an hour.
The air was blurred with dry leaves flying,
Gold and scarlet, gaily dying.
A squirrel ran off with a nut in his mouth,
And always, always, flying south,
Twittering, the birds went by
Flickering sharp against the sky,
Some in great bows, some in wedges,
Some in bands with wavering edges;
Flocks and flocks were flying over
With the north wind for their drover.
'Flowers,' I said, 'You'd better go,
Surely it's coming on for snow!' —
They did not heed me, nor heed the birds,
Twittering thin, far-fallen words —
The others thought of tomorrow, but they
Only remembered yesterday.

— Sara Teasdale

NOVEMBER SKIES

Than these November skies
Is no sky lovelier. The clouds are deep;
Into their grey the subtle spies
Of colour creep,
Changing that high austerity to delight,
Till ev'n the leaden interfolds are bright.
And, where the cloud breaks, faint far azure peers
Ere a thin flushing cloud again
Shuts up that loveliness, or shares.
The huge great clouds move slowly, gently, as
Reluctant the quick sun should shine in vain,
Holding in bright caprice their rain.
   And when of colours none,
Nor rose, nor amber, nor the scarce late green,
Is truly seen, —
In all the myriad grey,
In silver height and dusky deep, remain
The loveliest,
Faint purple flushes of the unvanquished sun.

— John Freeman

♪ THE SOULING SONG

Sung on All Soul's Day, November first

A soul! a soul! a soul-cake!
Please, good Missis, a soul-cake!
An apple, a pear, a plum, or a cherry,
Any good thing to make us all merry,
One for Peter, two for Paul,
Three for Him who made us all.

257

God bless the master of this house,
　　The misteress also,
And all the little children
　　That round your table grow.
Likewise young men and maidens,
　　Your cattle and your store;
And all that dwells within your gates,
　　We wish you ten times more.

Down into the cellar,
　　And see what you can find,
If the barrels are not empty,
　　We hope you will prove kind.
(We hope you will prove kind,
　　With your apples and strong beer,
And we'll come no more a-souling
　　Till this time next year.)

The lanes are very dirty,
　　My shoes are very thin,
I've got a little pocket
　　To put a penny in.
If you haven't got a penny,
　　A ha'penny will do;
If you haven't got a ha'penny,
　　It's God bless you!

A soul! a soul! a soul-cake!
Please, good Missis, a soul-cake!
An apple, a pear, a plum, or a cherry,
Any good thing to make us all merry,
One for Peter, two for Paul,
Three for Him who made us all.

— Traditional: English

SAINT CLEMENT'S DAY

November twenty-third

Clemany! Clemany! Clemany mine!
A good red apple, a pint of wine,
Some of your mutton and some of your veal,
If it is good, pray give me a deal.
An apple, a pear, a plum or a cherry,
Any good thing to make us merry;
A bouncing buck and a velvet chair,
Clemany comes but once a year.
Off with the pot and on with the pan;
A good red apple, and I'll be gone.

— Traditional: English

CAROL

Winter winds have chilled us quite —
  With a hey! for the goose, and the holly berry red:
Out in the snow-white, starlit night,
    Sorry waifs are we that have long an-hungerèd,
      Yet can still sing loud and true,
      With 'Good even, Sirs, to you,'
All for a small Stranger's sake that no cradle knew.

Winter winds have chilled our bones —
  With a hey! for the goose, and the bowl that bringeth
    cheer,
Sweet sirs, our feet are cold as stones,
    Sorry waifs are we, yet can still sing loud and clear,
      Yet can still sing loud and true,
      With 'Good even, Sirs, to you,'
All for a small Stranger's sake that no cradle knew.

— Hamish Maclaren

CAROL

Villagers all, this frosty tide,
Let your doors swing open wide,
Though wind may follow, and snow beside,
Yet draw us in by your fire to bide;
    Joy shall be yours in the morning!

Here we stand in the cold and the sleet,
Blowing fingers and stamping feet,
Come from far away you to greet —
You by the fire and we in the street —
    Bidding you joy in the morning!

For ere one half of the night was gone,
Sudden a star has led us on,
Raining bliss and benison —
Bliss tomorrow and more anon,
    Joy for every morning!

Goodman Joseph toiled through the snow —
Saw the star o'er a stable low;
Mary she might not further go —
Welcome thatch and litter below!
    Joy was hers in the morning!

And then they heard the angels tell
'Who were the first to cry Nowell?
Animals all, as it befell,
In the stable where they did dwell!
    Joy shall be theirs in the morning!'

                — *Kenneth Grahame*

from: *The Wind in the Willows*

𝄞 AS JOSEPH WAS A-WALKING

As Joseph was a-walking
He heard an angel sing:
'This night shall be the birth-night
Of Christ, the heavenly King.

'He neither shall be born
In housen nor in hall,
Nor in the place of Paradise,
But in the oxen's stall.

'He neither shall be rockèd
In silver nor in gold,
But in a wooden cradle
That rocks in the mould.

'He neither shall be washen
With white wine nor with red,
But with the fair spring water
With which we were christenèd.

'He neither shall be clothèd
In purple nor in pall,
But in the fair white linen
That usen babies all.'

As Joseph was a-walking
Thus did the angel sing,
And Mary's Son at midnight
Was born to be our King.

Mary took her Baby,
She dressed Him so sweet,
She laid Him in a manger,
All there for to sleep.

Then be you glad, good people,
At this time of the year,
And light you up your candles
For His star it shineth clear.

— Traditional: English

OLD CAROL

He came all so still
Where his mother was,
As dew in April
That falleth on the grass.

He came all so still
To his mother's bower,
As dew in April
That falleth on the flower.

He came all so still
Where his mother lay,
As dew in April
That falleth on the spray.

Mother and maiden
Was never none but she;
Well may such a lady
God's mother be.

— Unknown

♪ NEVER WAS A CHILD SO LOVELY

Never was a child so lovely
Born in ox's stall so lowly;
Ne'er was gift so great to earth
As God's gift, the Virgin Birth.

So the manger they could find,
Wise men were by star beshined,
And the shepherds prayed enow,
As their heads did humbly bow.

Child no crying he did make;
Angels' songs the silence break;
Came betimes the neighbors all,
Homage paying to the stall.

God ne'er seen by mannès eye
Silent sate fornent the sky,
Knowing though the angels sang,
His wee son on a cross would hang.

His wee son in man's estate
Come to a wrong-doer's fate,
Sinless die as lived he here,
Master, Saviour, Christ our dear.

Never was a child so lovely
Born in ox's stall so lowly;
Ne'er was gift so great to earth
As God's gift, the Virgin Birth.

— Traditional: American

Collected by *John Jacob Niles*

from: HYMN ON THE MORNING OF
CHRIST'S NATIVITY

It was the winter wild,
While the heaven-born child
   All meanly wrapt in rude manger lies;
Nature in awe to Him
Has dofft her gaudy trim,
   With her great Master so to sympathize:
It was no season then for her
To wanton with the sun, her lusty paramour.

   .   .   .   .

Nor war, or battle's sound
Was heard the world around:
   The idle spear and shield were high up hung,
The hookèd chariot stood
Unstained with hostile blood,
   The trumpet spake not to the armed throng,
The kings sat still with awful eye,
As if they surely knew their sov'reign Lord was by.

But peaceful was the night,
Wherein the Prince of light
   His reign of peace upon the earth began:
The winds with wonder whist
Smoothly the waters kist,
   Whispering new joys to the mild ocean,
Who now hath quite forgot to rave,
While birds of calm sit brooding on the charmèd wave.

The stars with deep amaze
Stand fixed with steadfast gaze,
   Bending one way their precious influence,

And will not take their flight,
For all the morning light,
　　Or Lucifer that often warned them thence;
But in their glimmering orbs did glow,
Until their Lord Himself bespake, and bid them go.

　.　　.　　.　　.　　.　　.　　.　　.　　.　　.　　.

The shepherds on the lawn,
Or ere the point of dawn,
　　Sat simply chatting in a rustic row;
Full little thought they then
That the mighty Pan
　　Was kindly come to live with them below;
Perhaps their loves, or else their sheep,
Was all that did their silly thoughts so busy keep.

But see the Virgin blest
Hath laid her Babe to rest,
　　Time is our tedious song should here have ending:
Heaven's youngest teemèd star
Hath fixed her polished car,
　　Her sleeping Lord with handmaid lamp attending;
And all about the courtly stable
Bright harnessed Angels sit in order serviceable.

— John Milton

JOLLY WAT

Can I not sing but 'Hoy,'
When the joly shepard made so much joy?

The shepard upon a hill he sat;
He had on him his tabard and his hat,
His tar-box, his pipe, and his flagat;
His name was callèd Joly Joly Wat,
   For he was a gud herdès boy.
        Ut hoy!
  For in his pipe he made so much joy.

The shepard upon a hill was laid;
His dog unto his girdell was taid;
He had not slept but a little braid
But *'Gloria in excelsis'* to him was said.
        Ut hoy!
  For in his pipe he made so much joy.

The shepard on a hill he stode;
Round about him his shepe they yode;
He put his hond under his hode,
He saw a star as rede as blode.
        Ut hoy!
  For in his pipe he made so much joy.

The shepard said anon right,
'I will go see yon ferly sight,

tabard: short coat.
flagat: flash.
braid: time.
yode: went.
ferly: wonderful.

Whereas an angel singeth on hight,
And the star that shineth so bright.'
                    Ut hoy!
        For in his pipe he made so much joy.

'Now farewell Mall, and also Will!
For my love go ye all still
Unto I cum again you till,
And evermore, Will, ring well thy bell.'
                    Ut hoy!
        For in his pipe he made so much joy.

'Now must I go where Crist was born;
Farewell! I cum again to-morn.
Dog, kepe well my shepe fro the corn,
And warn well "Warroke" when I blow my horn!'
                    Ut hoy!
        For in his pipe he made so much joy.

When Wat to Bedlem cumen was,
He swet, he had gone faster than a pace;
He found Jesu in a simpell place,
Between an ox but and an asse.
                    Ut hoy!
        For in his pipe he made so much joy.

Jesu, I offer to thee here my pipe,
My skirt, my tar-box, and my scrip;
Home to my fellowes now will I skip,
And also look unto my shepe.'
                    Ut hoy!
        For in his pipe he made so much joy.

'Now farewell, mine owne herdesman Wat!'
'Yea, for God, lady, even I hat;
Lull well Jesu in thy lap,
And farewell, Joseph, with thy round cap!'
    Ut hoy!
  For in his pipe he made so much joy.

'Now may I well both hope and sing,
For I have bene at Cristes bering;
Home to my felowes now will I fling.
Crist of Heaven to his bliss us bring!'
    Ut hoy!
  For in his pipe he made so much joy.

                    — *Traditional: English*

I hat: I am called.

♪ 'SOME SAY...'

Some say that ever 'gainst that season comes
Wherein our Savior's birth is celebrated,
The bird of dawning singeth all night long:
And then, they say, no spirit dare stir abroad,
The nights are wholesome, then no planets strike,
No fairy takes nor witch hath power to charm,
So hallow'd and so gracious is the time.

— *William Shakespeare*

from: *Hamlet,* Act I. Scene 1

♪ from: SHEPHERDS HYMN THEIR SAVIOUR

We saw Thee in Thy balmy nest,
Young dawn of our eternal day:
We saw Thine eyes break from the East
And chase the trembling shades away.
We saw Thee, and we blest the sight,
We saw Thee by Thine own sweet light.

Poor World, said I, what wilt thou do
To entertain this starry stranger?
Is this the best thou canst bestow —
A cold and none too cleanly manger?
Contend, ye powers of heaven and earth,
To fit a bed for this huge birth.

— *Richard Crashaw*

271

ALL MOTHERS SPEAK TO MARY

Send forth the star;
And, Mary, take His hand —
He may not understand
How changed we are.
Light towering candles, rim
The earth with them;
Let angels sing 'Amen'
To His birth-hymn.
Let Thy sweet laughter
When He was born
Fill this dark morn —
Sky-rafter to rafter.

Mary, thou canst see
Between the suns
The road that runs
From Manger to Calvary.
Let Him not fear our dole
Of hate and gall;
He is too small
For agony of soul.
Make then His coming bright
On earth; let every door
Swing wide with peace; nor
Let one evil thing blot out the night.

— Ruth Sawyer

A CAROL FOR CHILDREN

God rest you merry, Innocents,
Let nothing you dismay,
Let nothing wound an eager heart
Upon this Christmas day.

Yours be the genial holly wreaths,
The stockings and the tree;
An aged world to you bequeaths
Its own forgotten glee.

Soon, soon enough come crueler gifts,
The anger and the tears;
Between you now there sparsely drifts
A handful yet of years.

Oh, dimly, dimly glows the star
Through the electric throng;
The bidding in temple and bazaar
Drowns out the silver song.

The ancient altars smoke afresh,
The ancient idols stir;
Faint in the reek of burning flesh
Sink frankincense and myrrh.

Gaspar, Balthazar, Melchior!
Where are your offerings now?
What greetings to the Prince of War,
His darkly branded brow?

Two ultimate laws alone we know,
The ledger and the sword —

So far away, so long ago,
We lost the infant Lord.

Only the children clasp His hand;
His voice speaks low to them,
And still for them the shining band
Wings over Bethlehem.

God rest you merry, Innocents,
While Innocence endures.
A sweeter Christmas than we to ours
May you bequeath to yours.

— *Ogden Nash*

THE SHEPHERD AND THE KING

The Shepherd and the King,
The Angel and the Ass,
They heard Sweet Mary sing
When her joy was come to pass;
They heard Sweet Mary sing
To the Baby on her knee;
Sing again, Sweet Mary,
And we will sing with thee!
　　Earth, bear a berry!
　　Heaven, bear a light!
　　Man, make you merry
　　On Christmas Night.

The Oxen in the stall,
The Sheep upon the hill,
They are waking all
To hear Sweet Mary still.

The Baby is a Child,
And the Child is running free;
Sing again, Sweet Mary,
And we will sing with thee!
    Earth, bear a berry!
    Heaven, bear a light!
    Man, make you merry
    On Christmas night.

The People in the land,
So many million strong,
All silently do stand
To hear Sweet Mary's song.
The Child He is a Man,
And the Man hangs on a tree.
Sing again, Sweet Mary,
And we will sing with thee!
    Earth, bear a berry!
    Heaven, bear a light!
    Man, make you merry
    On Christmas night.

The Stars that are so old,
The Grass that is so young,
They listen in the cold
To hear Sweet Mary's tongue.
The Man's the Son of God,
And in Heaven walketh He.
Sing again, Sweet Mary,
And we will sing with thee!
    Earth, bear a berry!
    Heaven, bear a light!
    Man, make you merry
    On Christmas night.

            — Eleanor Farjeon

THE FOURTH SHEPHERD

The four strange men knelt down to see
  The Boy that sleeping lay,
And three were full of ecstasy,
  But one said, softly: 'Nay.'
And he that so denied went out
  Into the starry calm,
For, somewhere in the dark, he thought
  He heard a bleating lamb.
With heartstrings tight with pity, he
  Forgot the child within,
And Mary and his comrades three,
  And counted it no sin.
Back all the weary way he trod,
  And paused not once for sleep;
  'That child may be the Son of God,
  But I must guard my sheep!'

— *Alexander Mackenzie Davidson*

TO A CHILD

Go, pretty child, and bear this flower
   Unto thy little Saviour,
And tell him, by that bud now blown,
He is the Rose of Sharon known.
When thou hast said so, stick it there
Upon his bib or stomacher;
And tell him, for good handsel too,
That thou hast brought a whistle new,
Made of a clean straight oaten reed,
To charm his cries at time of need.
Tell him, for coral thou hast none,
But, if thou hadst, he should have one;
But poor thou art, and known to be
Even as moneyless as he.
Lastly, if thou canst win a kiss
From those mellifluous lips of his,
Then never take a second on,
To spoil the first impression.

— Robert Herrick

handsel: a gift, regarded as the first of a series.
coral: a plaything for a baby, usually a teething-ring, made of coral.

♪ I WASH MY FACE IN A GOLDEN VASE

I wash my face in a golden vase,·
　　All on a Christmas morning;
I wipe my face on a lily-white towel,
　　All on a Christmas day.

I comb my hair with an ivory comb,
　　All on a Christmas morning;
While two little ships were a-standing by,
　　All on a Christmas day.

Oh, guess who was in one of them,
　　All on a Christmas morning!
The Blessed Virgin and her Son,
　　All on a Christmas day.

Then God looked down and said 'twas well,
　　All on a Christmas morning,
'Now all my folks is saved from Hell.'
　　All on a Christmas day.

— Traditional: American

Collected by *John Jacob Niles*

♪ THE THREE SHIPS

As I sat under a sycamore-tree,
  A sycamore-tree, a sycamore-tree,
I looked me out upon the sea
  On Christ's Sunday at morn.

I saw three ships a-sailing there,
  A-sailing there, a-sailing there,
Jesu, Mary and Joseph they bare
  On Christ's Sunday at morn.

Joseph did whistle and Mary did sing,
  Mary did sing, Mary did sing,
And all the bells on earth did ring
  For joy our Lord was born.

O they sail'd into Bethlehem!
  To Bethlehem, to Bethlehem!
Saint Michael was the sterèsman,
  Saint John sat in the horn.

And all the bells on earth did ring,
  On earth did ring, on earth did ring;
'Welcome be thou, Heaven's King,
  On Christ's Sunday at morn!'

— Traditional: English

horn: prow.

THE ENDING OF THE YEAR

When trees did show no leaves,
   And grass no daisies had,
And fields had lost their sheaves,
   And streams in ice were clad,
And day of light was shorn,
   And wind had got a spear,
Jesus Christ was born
   In the ending of the year.

Like green leaves when they grow,
   He shall for comfort be;
Like life in streams shall flow,
   For running water He;
He shall raise hopes like corn
   For barren fields to bear,
And therefore He was born
   In the ending of the year.

Like daisies to the grass,
   His innocence He'll bring;
In keenest winds that pass
   His flowering love shall spring;
The rising of the morn
   At midnight shall appear,
Whenever Christ is born
   In the ending of the year.

— Eleanor Farjeon

CHRISTMAS EVE CEREMONY

I

Come guard this night the Christmas pie,
   That the thief, though ne'er so sly,
With his flesh-hooks don't come nigh
            To catch it
From him, who all alone sits there
Having his eyes still in his ear,
And a deal of nightly fear,
            To watch it.

II

Wassail the trees, that they may bear
You many a plum and many a pear:
For more or less fruits they will bring,
As you do give them wassailing.

— *Robert Herrick*

𝄞 THE KENTUCKY WASSAIL SONG

Wassail, wassail all over the town,
The cup is white and the ale is brown,
The cup is made from the old oak-tree,
And the ale is made in Kentucky,
So it's joy be to you and a jolly wassail!

Oh, good man and good wife, are you within?
Pray lift the latch and let us come in.
We see you a-sitting at the boot o' the fire,
Not a-thinkin' of us in the mud and the mire,
So it's joy be to you and a jolly wassail!

Oh, where is the servant with the silly little pin
To open the latch and let us come in?
For here in the draught hit is our desire
To nibble on a cheese and a toast by the fire,
So it's joy be to you and a jolly wassail!

There was an old maid and she lived in a house,
And she had for a pet a tiny wee mouse,
Oh, the house had a stove and the house was warm,
And a little bit of liquor won't do no harm,
So it's joy be to you and a jolly wassail!

Oh, a man in York drank his sack from a pail,
But all we ask is a wee wassail.
Ah, husband and wife, alack, we part,
God bless this house from the bottom of our heart,
So it's joy be to you and a jolly wassail!

— Traditional: American

Collected by *John Jacob Niles*

AN APPLE-TREE RHYME

To be Sung in Orchards, at the New Year

Here stands a good apple tree;
Stand fast at the root,
Bear well at top:
Every little twig
Bear an apple big;
Every little bough
Bear an apple now;
Hats full! caps full!
Three-score sacks full!
Hullo, boys! hullo!

— *Traditional: English*

A NEW YEAR CAROL

Here we bring new water
    from the well so clear,
For to worship God with,
    this happy New Year.
Sing levy dew, sing levy dew,
    the water and the wine;
The seven bright gold wires
    and the bugles that do shine.

Sing reign of Fair Maid,
    with gold upon her toe, —
Open you the West Door,
    and turn the Old Year go.

283

Sing reign of Fair Maid
    with gold upon her chin, —
Open you the East Door,
    and let the New Year in.
Sing levy dew, sing levy dew,
    the water and the wine;
The seven bright gold wires
    and the bugles they do shine.

— Traditional: English

AN ALMANAC

Our Elder Brother is a Spirit of Joy:
Therefore in this new year, Rejoice!

In January the Spirit Dreams,
And in February weaves a Rainbow,
And in March smiles through Rains,
And in April is clad in White and Green,
And in May is the Youth of the World,
And in June is a Glory,
And in July is in two Worlds,
And in August is a Colour,
And in September dreams of Beauty,
And in October Sighs,
And in November Wearieth,
And in December sleeps.

— Fiona Macleod (William Sharp)

284

A WISH

A glad New Year to all! —
Since many a tear,
Do what we can, must fall,
The greater need to wish a glad
        New Year.

Since lovely youth is brief,
O girl and boy,
And no one can escape a share of grief,
I wish you joy;

Since hate is with us still,
I wish men love;
I wish, since hovering hawks still strike to kill,
The coming of the dove;

And since the ghouls of terror and despair
Are still abroad,
I wish the world once more within the care
Of those who have seen God.

             — *Eleanor Farjeon*

♪ CEREMONIES FOR CANDLEMASSE EVE

Down with the rosemary and bays,
  Down with the mistletoe;
Instead of holly, now upraise
  The greener box for show.

The holly hitherto did sway;
  Let box now domineer;
Until the dancing Easter-day,
  Or Easter's eve appear.

Then youthful box which now hath grace,
  Your houses to renew;
Grown old, surrender must his place,
  Unto the crisped yew.

When yew is out, then birch comes in,
  And many flowers beside;
Both of a fresh and fragrant kin
  To honour Whitsuntide.

Green rushes then, and sweetest bents,
  With cooler oaken boughs;
Come in for comely ornaments
  To re-adorn the house.
Thus times do shift; each thing his turn does hold;
New things succeed, as former things grow old.

— *Robert Herrick*

bents: grasses.

UPON CANDLEMASSE DAY

End now the white loaf and the pie,
And let all sports with Christmas die.

— *Robert Herrick*

𝄞 MERRY ARE THE BELLS

Merry are the bells, and merry would they ring,
  Merry was myself, and merry would I sing;
With a merry ding-dong, happy, gay and free,
  And a merry sing-song, happy let us be.

Waddle goes your gait, and hollow are your hose;
  Noddle goes your pate, and purple is your nose;
Merry is your sing-song, happy, gay and free;
  With a merry ding-dong, happy let us be.

Merry have we met, and merry have we been;
  Merry let us part, and merry meet again;
With a merry sing-song, happy, gay and free;
  With a merry ding-dong, happy let us be.

— Traditional: English

THE BELLS

I

Pancakes and fritters,
Say the bells of Saint Peter's.
Where must we fry 'em?
Say the bells of Cold Higham.
In yonder land furrow,
Say the bells of Wellingborough.
You owe me a shilling,
Say the bells of Great Billing.
When will you pay me?
Say the bells of Middleton Cheney.
When I am able,
Say the bells of Dunstable.
That will never be,
Say the bells of Coventry.
O yes it will,
Says Northampton great bell.

II

Three crows on a tree,
Say the bells of Oswestry;

Roast beef, and be merry,
Say the bells of Shrewsbury.

Three gold canaries,
Say the bells of Saint Mary's.

A boiling pot and a stewing pan,
Say the bells of Saint Julian.

You're a rogue for sartin,
Say the bells of Saint Martin.

Ivy, holly and mistletoe,
Say the bells of Wistanstow.

— *Traditional: English*

♪ THE BELLS OF LONDON

Gay go up and gay go down,
To ring the bells of London town.
  Halfpence and farthings,
  Say the bells of Saint Martin's,
    Oranges and lemons,
    Say the bells of Saint Clement's.
  Pancakes and fritters,
  Say the bells of Saint Peter's.
    Two sticks and an apple
    Say the bells of Whitechapel.
Kettles and pans,
Say the bells of Saint Ann's.
  You owe me ten shillings,
  Say the bells of Saint Helen's.
    When will you pay me?
    Say the bells of Old Bailey.
  When I grow rich,
  Say the bells of Shoreditch.
Pray when will that be?
Say the bells of Stepney.
  I am sure I don't know,
  Says the great bell of Bow.

— *Traditional: English*

THE CHILDREN'S BELLS

(When the muted City Bells of London were rung in com-
memoration of the Bell-Ringers who lost their lives in the
First World War, the bells of Saint Clement Danes in the
Strand could not join in because of a defect in the structure.)

Where are your Oranges?
Where are your Lemons?
What, are you silent now,
Bells of St. Clements?
You, of all bells that rang
Once in old London,
You, of all bells that sang,
Utterly undone?
You whom all children know
Ere they know letters,
Making Big Ben himself
Call you his betters?
Where are your lovely tones
Fruitful and mellow,
Full-flavoured orange-gold,
Clear lemon-yellow?
Ring again, sing again,
Bells of St. Clements!
Call as you swing again,
'Oranges! Lemons!'
Fatherless children
Are listening near you —
Sing for the children,
The fathers will hear you.

— *Eleanor Farjeon*

THE LITTLE BLACK BOY

My mother bore me in the southern wild,
   And I am black, but O my soul is white!
White as an angel is the English child,
   But I am black, as if bereaved of light.

My mother taught me underneath a tree,
   And, sitting down before the heat of day,
She took me on her lap and kissèd me,
   And, pointing to the East began to say;

'Look on the rising sun: there God does live,
   And gives His light, and gives His heat away,
And flowers and trees and beasts and men receive
   Comfort in morning, joy in the noonday.

'And we are put on earth a little space
   That we may learn to bear the beams of love;
And these black bodies and this sunburnt face
   Are but a cloud, and like a shady grove.

'For, when our souls have learned the heat to bear,
   The cloud will vanish, we shall hear His voice
Saying, "Come out from the grove, my love and care,
   And round my golden tent like lambs rejoice." '

Thus did my mother say, and kissèd me,
   And thus I say to little English boy.
When I from black, and he from white cloud free,
   And round the tent of God like lambs we joy,

I'll shade him from the heat till he can bear
   To lean in joy upon our Father's knee;
And then I'll stand and stroke his silver hair,
   And be like him, and he will then love me.

— *William Blake*

MOTHER TO SON

Well, son, I'll tell you:
Life for me ain't been no crystal stair.
It's had tacks in it,
And splinters,
And boards torn up,
And places with no carpet on the floor —
Bare.
But all the time
I'se been a-climbin' on,
And reachin' landin's,
And turnin' corners,
And sometimes goin' in the dark
Where there ain't been no light.
So, boy, don't you turn back;
Don't you set down on the steps
'Cause you find it kinder hard.
Don't you fall now —
For I'se still goin', honey,
I'se still climbin',
And life for me ain't been no crystal stair.

— *Langston Hughes*

AFTERWARDS

When the Present has latched its postern behind my trem-
    ulous stay,
  And the May month flaps its glad green leaves like wings
Delicate-filmed as new-spun silk, will the neighbours say,
   'He was a man who used to notice such things'?

If it be in the dusk when, like an eyelid's soundless blink,
  The deyfall-hawk comes crossing the shades to alight
Upon the wind-warped upland thorn, a gazer may think,
   'To him this must have been a familiar sight.'

If I pass during some nocturnal blackness, mothy and warm,
  When the hedgehog travels furtively over the lawn,
One may say, 'He strove that such innocent creatures should
    come to no harm,
  But he could do little for them; and now he is gone.'

If, when hearing that I have been stilled at last, they stand
    at the door,
  Watching the full-starred heavens that winter sees,
Will this thought rise on those who will meet my face no
    more,
   'He was one who had an eye for such mysteries?'

And will any say when my bell of quittance is heard in
    the gloom,
  And a crossing breeze cuts a pause in its outrollings,
Till they rise again, as they were a new bell's boom,
   'He hears it not now, but used to notice such things?'

                    — *Thomas Hardy*

FARE WELL

When I lie where shades of darkness
Shall no more assail mine eyes,
Nor the rain make lamentation
        When the wind sighs;
How will fare the world whose wonder
Was the very proof of me?
Memory fades, must the remembered
        Perishing be?

Oh, when this my dust surrenders
Hand, foot, lip, to dust again,
May those loved and loving faces
        Please other men!
May the rustling harvest hedgerow
Still the Traveller's Joy entwine,
And as happy children gather
        Posies once mine.

Look thy last on all things lovely,
Every hour. Let no night
Seal thy sense in deathly slumber
        Till to delight
Thou have paid thy utmost blessing;
Since that all things thou wouldst praise
Beauty took from those who loved them
        In other days.

— *Walter de la Mare*

'THE NIGHT IS FREEZING FAST'

The night is freezing fast,
   Tomorrow comes December;
     And winterfalls of old
Are with me from the past;
   And chiefly I remember
     How Dick would hate the cold.

Fall, winter, fall; for he,
   Prompt hand and headpiece clever,
     Has woven a winter robe,
And made of earth and sea
   His overcoat forever,
     And wears the turning globe.

— A. E. Housman

♯ AN OLD WOMAN OF THE ROADS

Oh, to have a little house!
   To own the hearth and stool and all!
The heaped-up sods upon the fire,
   The pile of turf against the wall!

To have a clock with weights and chains
   And pendulum swinging up and down,
A dresser filled with shining delph,
   Speckled white and blue and brown!

I could be busy all the day
   Clearing and sweeping hearth and floor,
And fixing on their shelf again
   My white and blue and speckled store!

I could be quiet there at night
   Beside the fire and by myself,
Sure of a bed, and loth to leave
   The ticking clock and the shining delph!

Och! but I'm weary of mist and dark,
   And roads where there's never a house or bush,
And tired I am of bog and road
   And the crying wind and the lonesome hush!

And I am praying to God on high,
   And I am praying him night and day,
For a little house, a house of my own —
   Out of the wind's and the rain's way.

— Padraic Colum

TWO WOMEN UNDER A MAPLE

I came around a corner of a day
Expecting to find more brown men making hay,
For haying time was at its highest tide
And men too busy to let the small boys ride;
The sun was up ten minutes of twelve o'clock —
It was no time for tales or love or talk.

And two wives cool as summer wives can be
Were playing checkers under a maple tree.
They had white aprons on and sleeves rolled high
As if they had just left an apple pie;
Shade and sunlight polka-dotted their faces,
They moved their checkers with no airs or graces.
There they sat refuting, square of chin,
That resting is New England's cardinal sin.

— Robert P. Tristram Coffin

MENDING WALL

Something there is that doesn't love a wall,
That sends the frozen-ground-swell under it,
And spills the upper boulders in the sun;
And makes gaps even two can pass abreast.
The work of hunters is another thing:
I have come after them and made repair
Where they have left not one stone on a stone,
But they would have the rabbit out of hiding,
To please the yelping dogs. The gaps I mean,
No one has seen them made or heard them made,
But at spring mending-time we find them there.
I let my neighbour know beyond the hill;
And on a day we meet to walk the line
And set the wall between us once again.
We keep the wall between us as we go.
To each the boulders that have fallen to each.
And some are loaves and some so nearly balls
We have to use a spell to make them balance:
'Stay where you are until our backs are turned!'
We wear our fingers rough with handling them.
Oh, just another kind of out-door game,
One on a side. It comes to little more:
There where it is we do not need the wall:
He is all pine and I am apple orchard.
My apple trees will never get across
And eat the cones under his pines, I tell him.
He only says, 'Good fences make good neighbours.'
Spring is the mischief in me, and I wonder
If I could put a notion in his head:
'*Why* do they make good neighbours? Isn't it
Where there are cows? But here there are no cows.

Before I built a wall I'd ask to know
What I was walling in or walling out,
And to whom I was like to give offence.
Something there is that doesn't love a wall,
That wants it down.' I could say 'Elves' to him,
But it's not elves exactly, and I'd rather
That he said it for himself. I see him there
Bringing a stone grasped firmly by the top
In each hand, like an old-stone savage armed.
He moves in darkness as it seems to me,
Not of woods only and the shade of trees.
He will not go behind his father's saying,
And he likes having thought of it so well
He says again, 'Good fences make good neighbours.'

— *Robert Frost*

TO A FAT LADY SEEN FROM THE TRAIN

O why do you walk through the fields in gloves,
  Missing so much and so much?
O fat white woman whom nobody loves,
Why do you walk through the fields in gloves,
When the grass is soft as the breast of doves
  And shivering-sweet to the touch?
O why do you walk through the fields in gloves,
  Missing so much and so much?

— *Frances Cornford*

MISSOURI

A little clearing on the mountain side,
Brown earth, brown mule, brown cabin, lean brown dogs;
A wreath of redbud and a wild plum bride
With April rain accompanying young frogs
In whistling choruses and odes to spring;
The brown mule sneers and casts a scornful eye
To where on track below a monster thing
Awaits another monster thundering by.
His mistress' calico, full-skirted swings
As with a telling stroke she wields the hoe,
Scant time she has for brides and frogs and things.
Potatoes will be sprouting soon, you know;
Nor does she heed the watchers in the train —
This wide old woman — hoeing in the rain.

— *Caroline Lawrence Dier*

MRS. REECE LAUGHS

Laughter, with us, is no great undertaking,
A sudden wave that breaks and dies in breaking.
Laughter with Mrs. Reece is much less simple:
It germinates, it spreads, dimple by dimple,
From small beginnings, things of easy girth,
To formidable redundancies of mirth.
Clusters of subterranean chuckles rise,
And presently the circles of her eyes
Close into slits, and all the woman heaves
As a great elm with all its mound of leaves
Wallows before the storm. From hidden sources
A mustering of blind volcanic forces
Takes her and shakes her till she sobs and gapes.
Then all that load of bottled mirth escapes
In one wild crow, a lifting of huge hands,
And creaking stays, and visage that expands
In scarlet ridge and furrow. Thence collapse,
A hanging head, a feeble hand that flaps
An apron end to stir an air and waft
A steaming face. And Mrs. Reece has laughed.

— *Martin Armstrong*

BERRIES

There was an old woman
  Went blackberry picking
Along the hedges
  From Weep to Wicking.
Half a pottle —
  No more had she got,
When out steps a Fairy
  From her green grot;
And says, 'Well, Jill,
  Would 'ee pick 'ee mo?'
And Jill, she curtseys,
  And looks just so.
'Be off,' says the Fairy,
  'As quick as you can,
Over the meadows
  To the little green lane,
That dips to the hayfields
  Of Farmer Grimes:
I've berried those hedges
  A score of times;
Bushel on bushel
  I'll promise 'ee, Jill,
This side of supper
  If 'ee pick with a will.'
She glints very bright,
  And speaks her fair;
Then lo, and behold!
  She had faded in the air.

Be sure Old Goodie
  She trots betimes

Over the meadows
    To Farmer Grimes.
And never was queen
    With jewellery rich
As those same hedges
    From twig to ditch;
Like Dutchmen's coffers,
    Fruit, thorn and flower —
They shone like William
    And Mary's bower.
And be sure Old Goodie
    Went back to Weep,
So tired with her basket
    She scarce could creep.
When she comes in the dusk
    To her cottage door,
There's Towser wagging
    As never before,
To see his Missus
    So glad to be,
Come from her fruit-picking
    Back to he.

As soon as next morning
    Dawn was grey,
The pot on the hob
    Was simmering away;
And all in a stew
    And a hugger-mugger
Towser and Jill
    A-boiling of sugar,
And the dark clear fruit
    That from Faërie came,

For syrup and jelly
  And blackberry jam.

Twelve jolly gallipots
  Jill put by;
And one little teeny one
  One inch high;
And that she's hidden
  A good thumb deep,
Half way over
  From Wicking to Weep.

— *Walter de la Mare*

THE FIDDLERS

Nine feat fiddlers had good Queen Bess
To play her music as she did dress.
Behind an arras of horse and hound
They sate there scraping delightsome sound.
Spangled, bejewelled, her skirts would she
Draw o'er a petticoat of cramasie;
And soft each string like a bird would sing
In the starry dusk of evening.
Then slow from the deeps the crisscross bows,
Crooning like doves, arose and arose,
Till when, like a cage, her ladies did raise
A stiff rich splendour o'er her ribbed stays,
Like bumbling bees those four times nine
Fingers in melodies loud did pine;
Till came her coif and her violet shoon
And her virgin face shone out like the moon:

Oh, then in rapture those three times three
Fiddlers squealed shrill on their topmost C.

— Walter de la Mare

THE CUPBOARD

I know a little cupboard,
With a teeny tiny key,
And there's a jar of Lollypops
    For me, me, me.

It has a little shelf, my dear,
As dark as dark can be,
And there's a dish of Banbury Cakes
    For me, me, me.

I have a small fat grandmamma,
With a very slippery knee,
And she's Keeper of the Cupboard,
    With the key, key, key,

And when I'm very good, my dear,
As good as good can be,
There's Banbury Cakes, and Lollypops
    For me, me, me.

— Walter de la Mare

SEUMAS BEG

A man was sitting underneath a tree
Outside the village; and he asked me what
Name was upon this place; and said that he
Was never here before — He told a lot

Of stories to me too. His nose was flat!
I asked him how it happened, and he said
— The first mate of the Holy Ghost did that
With a marling-spike one day; but he was dead,

And jolly good job too; and he'd have gone
A long way to have killed him — Oh, he had
A gold ring in one ear; the other one
— 'Was bit off by a crocodile, bedad!' —

That's what he said. He taught me how to chew!
He was a real nice man! He liked me too!

— James Stephens

BREAKFAST TIME

The sun is always in the sky
Whenever I get out of bed,
And I often wonder why
It's never late. — My sister said

She didn't know who did the trick,
And that she didn't care a bit,
And I should eat my porridge quick,
. . . I think its mother wakens it.

— James Stephens

'WE WHO WERE BORN'

We who were born
In country places
Far from cities
And shifting faces,
We have a birthright
No man can sell,
And a secret joy
No man can tell.

For we are kindred
To lordly things:
The wild duck's flight
And the white owl's wings,
The pike and the salmon,
The bull and the horse,
The curlew's cry
And the smell of gorse.

Pride of trees,
Swiftness of streams,
Magic of frost
Have shaped our dreams.
No baser vision
Their spirit fills
Who walk by right
On the naked hills.

— *Eiluned Lewis*

from: *Dew on the Grass*

♭ MY HEART'S IN THE HIGHLANDS

My heart's in the Highlands, my heart is not here;
My heart's in the Highlands a-chasing the deer;
Chasing the wild deer, and following the roe,
My heart's in the Highlands wherever I go.
Farewell to the Highlands, farewell to the North,
The birthplace of valour, the country of worth;
Wherever I wander, wherever I rove,
The Hills of the Highlands for ever I love.

Farewell to the mountains high covered with snow;
Farewell to the straths and green valleys below;
Farewell to the forests and wild-hanging woods;
Farewell to the torrents and loud-pouring floods;
My heart's in the Highlands, my heart is not here,
My heart's in the Highlands a-chasing the deer;
Chasing the wild deer, and following the roe,
My heart's in the Highlands wherever I go.

— *Robert Burns*

THE LAKE ISLE OF INNISFREE

I will arise and go now, and go to Innisfree,
 And a small cabin build there, of clay and wattles made;
Nine bean rows will I have there, a hive for the honey bee,
 And live alone in the bee-loud glade.

And I shall have some peace there, for peace comes drop-
  ping slow,
 Dropping from the veils of the morning to where the
  cricket sings;
There midnight's all a glimmer, and noon a purple glow,
 And evening full of the linnet's wings.

I will arise and go now, for always night and day
 I hear lake water lapping with low sounds by the shore;
While I stand on the roadway, or on the pavements gray,
 I hear it in the deep heart's core.

         — William Butler Yeats

HOMESICKNESS

It is sorrow to me not to be there
In the Rio Grande country where I belong,
Not to hear in March the drip of snow water,
To see the willows redden and the river greening,
Nor to watch in April at Peña Blanca
The wild plums blossom in a quick white storm.
Not to see the cut logs leaping
In the summer freshet of Peñasco water,
And the girls at Taos gathering plums in August,
The bent boughs leaning to the strong brown arms.
Sorrow it is not to see the aspen money flying
Like curdled gold strained through the keen bright air,
Or at Chimayó the chile drying
Till the walls of houses all come toward you
With the warm approaching red.
Oh, sorrow any time not to be there
In the Rio Grande country where I was bred!

— *Mary Austin*

'You may lie awake all night and never feel the passing of evil presences, nor hear printless feet; neither do you lapse into slumber with the comfortable consciousness of those friendly watchers who sit invisibly by a lonely sleeper under an English sky. Even an Irishman would not see a row of little men with green caps leaping along beneath the fireweed and the golden daisies; nor have the subtler fairies of England found these wilds. . . . The maple and the birch conceal no dryads, and Pan has never been heard among these reed beds. Look as long as you like upon a cataract of the New World, you shall not see a white arm rise from the foam.' *Rupert Brooke, in 'Letters from America.'*

WESTERN MAGIC

There are no fairy-folk in our Southwest,
The cactus spines would tear their filmy wings,
There's no dew anywhere for them to drink
And no green grass to make them fairy rings.

But sometimes in a windless blur of dust
The impish twins of War and Chance go by,
Or after storms the Spider Woman mends
With thin drawn cloud, torn edges of the sky.

And there is one who plays upon the flute
In deep rock crevices where springs are found, —
'Twas at To-yallanne they saw him first, —
In April youths are magicked by the sound.

Hot dawns the turquoise horse, Johano-ai,
Races the sun in dust of glittering grains,
Or round Pelado Peak the Rainbow Boy
Goes dancing with the many-footed rains.

There are no fairy-folk in our Southwest,
But there are hours when prairie-dog and snake,
Black beetle and the tecolote owl
Between two winks their ancient forms will take,

Clad in white skins with shell shield glittering,
The sun, their chief, the Ancient road will walk,
Half in her sleep the mothering earth
Of older things than fairy-folk will talk.

— *Mary Austin*

'ROADS GO EVER EVER ON'

Roads go ever ever on,
  Over rock and under tree,
By caves where sun has never shone,
  By streams that never find the sea;
Over snow by winter sown,
  And through the merry flowers of June,
Over grass and over stone,
  And under mountains in the moon.

Roads go ever ever on
  Under cloud and under star,
Yet feet that wandering have gone
  Turn at last to home afar.
Eyes that fire and sword have seen
  And horror in the halls of stone
Look at last on meadows green
  And trees and hills they long have known.

— *J. R. R. Tolkien*

from: *The Hobbit*

♪ CHRISTMAS

A Boy was born at Bethlehem
    that knew the haunts of Galilee;
He wandered on Mount Lebanon,
    and learned to love each forest tree.

But I was born at Marlborough,
    and love the homely faces there;
and for all other men besides
    'tis little love I have to spare.

I should not mind to die for them,
    my own dear downs, my comrades true;
But that great heart of Bethlehem,
    he died for men he never knew.

And yet, I think, at Golgotha,
    as Jesus' eyes were closed in death,
they saw with love most passionate
    the village streets at Nazareth.

             — *E. Hilton Young*

H.M.S. *Iron Duke,* 1914

from: THE WATER BABIES

When all the world is young, lad,
  And all the trees are green;
And every goose a swan, lad,
  And every lass a queen;
Then hey for boot and horse, lad,
  And round the world away:
Young blood must have its course, lad,
  And every dog his day.

When all the world is old, lad,
  And all the trees are brown;
And all the sport is stale, lad,
  And all the wheels run down;
Creep home, and take your place there,
  The spent and maimed among:
God grant you find one face there,
  You loved when all was young.

— Charles Kingsley

St. PAUL

If there be any
VIRTUE
and if there be any
PRAISE
Think on these
things

N.S.U

SONNET

There was an Indian, who had known no change,
Who strayed content along a sunlit beach
Gathering shells. He heard a sudden strange
Commingled noise; looked up; and gasped for speech.
For in the bay, where nothing was before,
Moved on the sea, by magic, huge canoes,
With bellying cloths on poles, and not one oar,
And fluttering coloured signs and clambering crews.

And he, in fear, this naked man alone,
His fallen hands forgetting all their shells,
His lips gone pale, knelt low behind a stone,
And stared, and saw, and did not understand,
Columbus's doom-burdened caravels
Slant to the shore, and all their seamen land.

— J. C. Squire

SQUARE-TOED PRINCES

My ancestors were fine, long men,
   Their hands were like square sails,
They ran the lengths of longitudes,
   Harpooning spouting whales.

Men to put a twinkle in
   The proud eyes of their Maker,
Standing up against the winds
   On the square toes of a Quaker.

From Baffin's Bay and Davis Strait
   To the Serpent of the South,
They had the whale-gaff in the fist
   And Scripture in the mouth.

Fingers like belaying pins,
   A heart like an iron bucket,
Humble servants of the Lord,
   Princes of Nantucket.

The wallowing mammoths of the sea
   Felt their ruddy will
And quaked along the Torrid Line
   From Gold Coast to Brazil.

In notches on the mizzen-mast
   These men kept the tally;
Their hearts were the Rose of Sharon
   And the Lily of the Valley.

The Yankee grit was in their spines,
 Their voices were like guns;
They yearned to breed a nation up,
 They manned their ships with sons.

They brought home ambergris and oil
 In hogsheads and in tierces
And knelt down on their pineboard floors
 To thank God for his mercies.

Square-riggers were their trundle-beds,
 And they found their graves
In the sea or nigh the sea,
 Within the sound of waves.

They wrapped the ocean like a cloak
 And the shifting dunes above them;
They lie in peace till the Judgment Day
 When the Lord will rise and love them.

— *Robert P. Tristram Coffin*

THE DICK JOHNSON REEL

Old Dick Johnson, gentleman, adventurer,
Braggart, minstrel, lover of a brawl,
Walked in the timber from Northfield to Hudson.
(Backward, forward and sashay all!)
Old Dick Johnson, joker and wanderer,
Poet, vagabond and beater of the track,
Sang a song of his bravery and prowess:
(Ladies go forward and gents go back!)

> Chorus:　Ripsi, rantsi,
> Humpsy, dumpsy;
> I, Dick Johnson,
> Killed Tecumseh!

Old Dick Johnson, fighter of the Indians,
Sang from Boston to the hills of Bath;
Sang the song of his muscle and his musket;
(Swing your partners and leave a path!)
The redskin sleeps where the wheat is growing,
But old Dick Johnson's ghost is free,
And it sings all night from Richfield to Twinsburg:
(All hands round with a one-two-three!)

> Chorus:　Ripsi, rantsi,
> Humpsy, dumpsy;
> I, Dick Johnson,
> Killed Tecumseh!

— *Jake Falstaff*

THE BALLAD OF WILLIAM SYCAMORE

1790–1871

My father, he was a mountaineer,
His fist was a knotty hammer;
He was quick on his feet as a running deer,
And he spoke with a Yankee stammer.

My mother, she was merry and brave,
And so she came to her labor,
With a tall green fir for her doctor grave
And a stream for her comforting neighbor.

And some are wrapped in the linen fine,
And some like a godling's scion;
But I was cradled on twigs of pine
And the skin of a mountain lion.

And some remember a white, starched lap
And a ewer with silver handles;
But I remember a coonskin cap
And the smell of bayberry candles.

The cabin logs, with the bark still rough,
And my mother who laughed at trifles,
And the tall, lank visitors, brown as snuff,
With their long, straight squirrel-rifles.

I can hear them dance, like a foggy song,
Through the deepest one of my slumbers,
The fiddle squeaking the boots along
And my father calling the numbers.

The quick feet shaking the puncheon-floor,
And the fiddle squealing and squealing,
Till the dried herbs rattled above the door
And the dust went up to the ceiling.

There are children lucky from dawn till dusk,
But never a child so lucky!
For I cut my teeth on 'Money Musk'
In the Bloody Ground of Kentucky!

When I grew tall as the Indian corn,
My father had little to lend me,
But he gave me his great, old powder-horn
And his woodsman's skill to befriend me.

With a leather shirt to cover my back,
And a redskin nose to unravel
Each forest sign, I carried my pack
As far as a scout could travel.

Till I lost my boyhood and found my wife,
A girl like a Salem clipper!
A woman straight as a hunting-knife
With eyes as bright as the Dipper!

We cleared our camp where the buffalo feed,
Unheard-of streams were our flagons;
And I sowed my sons like the apple-seed
On the trail of the Western wagons.

They were right, tight boys, never sulky or slow,
A fruitful, a goodly muster.
The eldest died at the Alamo.
The youngest fell with Custer.

The letter that told it burned my hand.
Yet we smiled and said, 'So be it!'
But I could not live when they fenced my land,
For it broke my heart to see it.

I saddled a red, unbroken colt
And rode him into the day there;
And he threw me down like a thunderbolt
And rolled on me as I lay there.

The hunter's whistle hummed in my ear
As the city-men tried to move me,
And I died in my boots like a pioneer
With the whole wide sky above me.

Now I lie in the heart of the fat, black soil,
Like the seed of a prairie-thistle;
It has ashed my bones with honey and oil
And picked them clean as a whistle.

And my youth returns, like the rains of Spring,
And my sons, like the wild-geese flying;
And I lie and hear the meadow-lark sing
And have much content in my dying.

Go play with the towns you have built of blocks,
The towns where you would have bound me!
I sleep in my earth like a tired fox,
And my buffalo have found me.

— Stephen Vincent Benét

328

A FARMER REMEMBERS LINCOLN

'Lincoln? —
Well, I was in the old Second Maine,
The first regiment in Washington from the Pine Tree State.
Of course I didn't get the butt of the clip;
We was there for guardin' Washington —
We was all green.

'I ain't never ben to the theayter in my life —
I didn't know how to behave.
I ain't never ben since.
I can see as plain as my hat the box where he sat in
When he was shot.
I can tell you, sir, there was a panic
When we found our President was in the shape he was in!
Never saw a soldier in the world but what liked him.

'Yes, sir. His looks was kind o' hard to forget.
He was a spare man,
An old farmer.
Everything was all right, you know,
But he wasn't a smooth-appearin' man at all —
Not in no ways;
Thin-faced, long-necked,
And a swellin' kind of a thick lip like.

'And he was a jolly old fellow — always cheerful;
He wasn't so high but the boys could talk to him their own
    ways.
While I was servin' at the Hospital
He'd come in and say, 'You look nice in here,'
Praise us up, you know.

And he'd bend over and talk to the boys —
And he'd talk so good to 'em — so close —
That's why I call him a farmer.
I don't mean that everything about him wasn't all right,
    you understand,
It's just — well, I was a farmer —
And he was my neighbor, anybody's neighbor.
I guess even you young folks would 'a' liked him.'

— Witter Bynner

ABRAHAM LINCOLN WALKS AT MIDNIGHT

(In Springfield, Illinois)

It is portentous and a thing of state
That here at midnight, in our little town
A mourning figure walks, and will not rest,
Near the old court-house pacing up and down.

Or by his homestead, or in shadowed yards
He lingers where his children used to play,
Or through the market, on the well-worn stones
He stalks until the dawn-stars burn away.

A bronzed, lank man! His suit of ancient black,
A famous high top-hat and plain worn shawl
Make him the quaint great figure that men love,
The prairie-lawyer, master of us all.

He cannot sleep upon his hillside now.
He is among us: — as in times before!
And we who toss and lie awake for long
Breathe deep, and start, to see him pass the door.

330

His head is bowed. He thinks on men and kings.
Yea, when the sick world cries, how can he sleep?
Too many peasants fight, they know not why,
Too many homesteads in black terror weep.

The sins of all the war-lords burn his heart.
He sees the dreadnoughts scouring every main.
He carries on his shawl-wrapped shoulders now
The bitterness, the folly and the pain.

He cannot rest until a spirit-dawn
Shall come: — the shining hope of Europe free:
The league of sober folk, the Workers' Earth,
Bringing long peace to Cornland, Alp and Sea.

It breaks his heart that kings must murder still,
That all his hours of travail here for men
Seem yet in vain. And who will bring white peace
That he may sleep upon his hill again?

— Vachel Lindsay

𝄞 NANCY HANKS
1784–1818

If Nancy Hanks
Came back as a ghost,
Seeking news
Of what she loved most,
She'd ask first
'Where's my son?
What's happened to Abe?
What's he done?

'Poor little Abe,
Left all alone
Except for Tom,
Who's a rolling stone;
He was only nine
The year I died.
I remember still
How hard he cried.

'Scraping along
In a little shack,
With hardly a shirt
To cover his back,
And a prairie wind
To blow him down,
Or pinching times
If he went to town.

'You wouldn't know
About my son?
Did he grow tall?
Did he have fun?
Did he learn to read?
Did he get to town?
Do you know his name?
Did he get on?'

— *Rosemary and Stephen Vincent Benét*

PIONEERS

A broken wagon wheel that rots away beside the river,
  A sunken grave that dimples on the bluff above the trail;
The larks call, the wind sweeps, the prairie grasses quiver
  And sing a wistful roving song of hoof and wheel and sail,
Pioneers, pioneers, you trailed it on to glory,
  Across the circling deserts to the mountains blue and dim.
New England was a night camp; Old England was a story,
  The new home, the true home, lay beyond the rim.

You fretted at the old hearth, the kettle and the cricket,
  The fathers' little acres, the wood lot and the pond.
Aye, better storm and famine and the arrow from the
    thicket,
    Along the trail to wider lands that glimmered out be-
      yond.
Pioneers, pioneers, the quicksands where you wallowed,
  The rocky hills and thirsty plains — they hardly won your
    heed.
You snatched the thorny chance, broke the trail that others
    followed,
  For sheer joy, for dear joy of marching in the lead.

Your wagon track is laid with steel; your tired dust is
    sleeping.
  Your spirit stalks the valleys where a restive nation teems.
Your soul has never left them in their sowing, in their
    reaping.
    The children of the outward trail, their eyes are full of
      dreams.

Pioneers, pioneers, your children will not reckon
   The dangers on the dusky ways no man has ever gone.
They look beyond the sunset where the better countries
     beckon,
   With old faith, with bold faith to find a wider dawn.

— Badger Clark

ULYSSES

It little profits that an idle king,
By this still hearth, among these barren crags,
Match'd with an aged wife, I mete and dole
Unequal laws unto a savage race,
That hoard, and sleep, and feed, and know not me.
I cannot rest from travel: I will drink
Life to the lees: all times I have enjoy'd
Greatly, have suffered greatly, both with those
That loved me, and alone; on shore, and when
Thro' scudding drifts the rainy Hyades
Vext the dim sea: I am become a name;
For always roaming with a hungry heart
Much have I seen and known, cities of men
And manners, climates, councils, governments,
Myself not least, but honour'd of them all;
And drunk delight of battle with my peers,
Far on the ringing plains of windy Troy.
I am a part of all that I have met;
Yet all experience is an arch wherethro'
Gleams that untravell'd world, whose margin fades
Forever and forever when I move.
How dull it is to pause, to make an end,
To rust unburnish'd, not to shine in use!

334

As tho' to breathe were life. Life piled on life
Were all too little, and of one to me
Little remains: but every hour is saved
From the eternal silence, something more,
A bringer of new things; and vile it were
For some three suns to store and hoard myself,
And this gray spirit yearning in desire
To follow knowledge, like a sinking star,
Beyond the utmost bound of human thought.
　　This is my son, mine own Telemachus,
To whom I leave the sceptre and the isle —
Well-loved of me, discerning to fulfil
This labour, by slow prudence to make mild
A rugged people, and thro' soft degrees
Subdue them to the useful and the good.
Most blameless is he, centred in the sphere
Of common duties, decent not to fail
In offices of tenderness, and pay
Meet adoration to my household gods,
When I am gone. He works his work, I mine.

　　There lies the port: the vessel puffs her sail:
There gloom the dark broad seas. My mariners,
Souls that have toil'd and wrought, and thought with me —
That ever with a frolic welcome took
The thunder and the sunshine, and opposed
Free hearts, free foreheads — you and I are old;
Old age hath yet his honour and his toil;
Death closes all; but something ere the end,
Some work of noble note, may yet be done,
Not unbecoming men that strove with Gods.
The lights begin to twinkle from the rocks;
The long day wanes: the slow moon climbs: the deep
Moans round with many voices. Come, my friends,

'Tis not too late to seek a newer world;
Push off, and sitting well in order smite
The sounding furrows; for my purpose holds
To sail beyond the sunset, and the baths
Of all the western stars, until I die.
It may be that the gulfs will wash us down:
It may be we shall touch the Happy Isles,
And see that great Achilles, whom we knew.
Tho' much is taken, much abides; and tho'
We are not now that strength which in old days
Moved earth and heaven; that which we are we are;
One equal temper of heroic hearts,
Made weak by time and fate, but strong in will
To strive, to seek, to find, and not to yield.

— *Alfred, Lord Tennyson*

MORTE D'ARTHUR

So all day long the noise of battle roll'd
Among the mountains by the winter sea,
Until King Arthur's table, man by man,
Had fallen in Lyonesse about their lord,
King Arthur; then, because his wound was deep,
The bold Sir Bedivere uplifted him,
Sir Bedivere, the last of all his knights,
And bore him to a chapel nigh the field,
A broken chancel with a broken cross,
That stood on a dark strait of barren land.
On one side lay the ocean, and on one
Lay a great water, and the moon was full.
  Then spake King Arthur to Sir Bedivere:
'The sequel of today unsolders all
The goodliest fellowship of famous knights
Whereof this world holds record. Such a sleep
They sleep — the men I loved. I think that we
Shall never more, at any future time,
Delight our souls with talk of knightly deeds,
Walking about the gardens and the halls
Of Camelot, as in the days that were.
I perish by this people which I made, —
Tho' Merlin sware that I should come again
To rule once more — but let what will be, be,
I am so deeply smitten thro' the helm
That without help I cannot last till morn.
Thou therefore take my brand Excalibur,
Which was my pride; for thou rememberest how
In those old days, one summer noon, an arm
Rose up from the bosom of the lake,
Clothed in white samite, mystic, wonderful,

Holding the sword — and how I row'd across
And took it, and have worn it, like a king;
And, wheresoever I am sung or told
In aftertime, this also shall be known.
But now delay not; take Excalibur,
And fling him far into the middle mere;
Watch what thou seëst, and lightly bring me word.'
    To him replied the bold Sir Bedivere:
'It is not meet, Sir King, to leave thee thus,
Aidless, alone, and smitten thro' the helm.
A little thing may harm a wounded man.
Yet I thy hest will all perform at full,
Watch what I see, and lightly bring thee word.'
    So saying, from the ruined shrine he stept
And in the moon athwart the place of tombs,
Where lay the mighty bones of ancient men,
Old knights, and over them the sea-wind sang
Shrill, chill, with flakes of foam. He, stepping down
By zig-zag paths and juts of pointed rock,
Came on the shining level of the lake.
    There drew he forth the brand Excalibur,
And o'er him, drawing it, the winter moon,
Brightening the skirts of a long cloud, ran forth
And sparkled keen with frost against the hilt;
For all the haft twinkled with diamond sparks,
Myriads of topaz-lights, and jacinth-work
Of subtlest jewellery. He gazed so long
That both his eyes were dazzled, as he stood,
This way and that dividing the swift mind,
In act to throw; but at the last it seem'd
Better to leave Excalibur conceal'd
There in the many-knotted water-flags,
That whistled stiff and dry about the marge.
So strode he back slow to the wounded king.

Then spake King Arthur to Sir Bedivere:
'Hast thou perform'd my mission which I gave thee?
What is it thou hast seen, or what hast heard?'
  And answer made the bold Sir Bedivere:
'I heard the ripple washing in the reeds,
And the wild water lapping on the crag.'
  To whom replied King Arthur, faint and pale:
'Thou hast betray'd thy nature and thy name,
Not rendering true answer, as beseem'd
Thy feälty, nor like a noble knight;
For surer sign had follow'd, either hand,
Or voice, or else a motion of the mere.
This is a shameful thing for men to lie.
Yet now I charge thee, quickly go again
As thou art lief and dear, and do the thing
I bade thee, watch, and lightly bring me word.'
  Then went Sir Bedivere the second time
Across the ridge, and paced beside the mere,
Counting the dewy pebbles, fix'd in thought;
But when he saw the wonder of the hilt,
How curiously and strangely chased, he smote
His palms together, and he cried aloud:
  'And if indeed I cast the brand away,
Surely a precious thing, one worthy note,
Should thus be lost forever from the earth,
Which might have pleased the eyes of many men.
What good should follow this, if this were done?
What harm, undone? Deep harm to disobey,
Seeing obedience is the bond of rule.
Were it well to obey then, if a king demand
An act unprofitable, against himself?
The king is sick, and knows not what he does.
What record, or what relic of my lord

339

Should be to aftertime, but empty breath
And rumours of a doubt? But were this kept,
Stored in some treasure-house of mighty kings,
Someone might show it at a joust of arms,
Saying, "King Arthur's sword, Excalibur,
Wrought by the lonely maiden of the lake;
Nine years she wrought it, sitting in the deeps
Upon the hidden bases of the hills."
So might some old man speak in the aftertime
To all the people, winning reverence;
But now much honour and much fame were lost.'

   So spake he, clouded with his own conceit,
And hid Excalibur the second time,
And so strode back slow to the wounded king.
   Then spoke King Arthur, breathing heavily:
'What is it thou hast seen, or what hast heard?'
   And answer made the bold Sir Bedivere:
'I heard the water lapping on the crag,
And the long ripple washing in the reeds.'
   To whom replied King Arthur, much in wrath:
'Ah, miserable and unkind, untrue,
Unknightly, traitor-hearted! Woe is me!
Authority forgets a dying king,
Laid widow'd of the power in his eye
That bow'd the will. I see thee what thou art,
For thou, the latest-left of all my knights,
In whom should meet the offices of all,
Thou wouldst betray me for the precious hilt;
Either from lust of gold, or like a girl
Valuing the giddy pleasures of the eyes.
Yet, for a man may fail in duty twice,
And the third time may prosper, get thee hence;
But, if thou spare to fling Excalibur,
I will arise and slay thee with my hands.'

Then quickly rose Sir Bedivere, and ran,
And, leaping down the ridges lightly, plunged
Among the bulrush-beds, and clutch'd the sword,
And strongly wheel'd and threw it. The great brand
Made lightnings in the splendour of the moon,
And flashing round and round, and whirl'd in an arch,
Shot like a streamer of the northern morn,
Seen where the moving isles of winter shock
By night, with noises of the northern sea.
So flash'd and fell the brand Excalibur:
But ere he dipt the surface, rose an arm
Clothed in white samite, mystic, wonderful,
And caught him by the hilt, and brandish'd him
Three times, and drew him under in the mere.
And lightly went the other to the King.
Then spoke King Arthur, drawing thicker breath:
'Now see I by thine eyes that this is done.
Speak out: what is it thou hast heard, or seen?'
And answer made the bold Sir Bedivere:
'Sir King, I closed mine eyelids, lest the gems
Should blind my purpose, for I never saw,
Nor shall I see, here or elsewhere, till I die,
Not tho' I live three lives of mortal men,
So great a miracle as yonder hilt.
Then with both hands I flung him, wheeling him;
But when I looked again, behold an arm,
Clothed in white samite, mystic, wonderful,
That caught him by the hilt, and brandish'd him
Three times, and drew him under in the mere.'

And answer made King Arthur, breathing hard:
'My end draws nigh; 'tis time that I were gone.
Make broad thy shoulders to receive my weight,
And bear me to the margin; yet I fear
My wound hath taken cold, and I shall die.'

341

So saying, from the pavement he half rose,
Slowly, with pain, reclining on his arm,
And looking wistfully with wide blue eyes
As in a picture. Him Sir Bedivere
Remorsefully regarded through his tears,
And would have spoken, but he found not words,
Then took with care, and kneeling on one knee,
O'er both his shoulders drew the languid hands,
And rising bore him thro' the place of tombs.

But, as he walk'd, King Arthur panted hard,
Like one that feels a nightmare on his bed
When all the house is mute. So sigh'd the King,
Muttering and murmuring at his ear 'Quick, quick!
I fear it is too late, and I shall die.'
But the other swiftly strode from ridge to ridge,
Clothed with his breath, and looking, as he walk'd,
Larger than human on the frozen hills.
He heard the deep behind him, and a cry
Before. His own thought drove him, like a goad.
Dry clash'd his harness in the icy caves
And barren chasms, and all to left and right
The bare black cliff clang'd round him, as he based
His feet on juts of slippery crag that rang
Sharp-smitten with the dint of armed heels —
And on a sudden, lo! the level lake,
And the long glories of the winter moon.

Then saw they how there hove a dusky barge,
Dark as a funeral scarf from stem to stern,
Beneath them; and descending they were ware
That all the decks were dense with stately forms,
Black-stoled, black-hooded, like a dream — by these
Three Queens with crowns of gold — and from them rose
A cry that shiver'd to the tingling stars,
And, as it were one voice, an agony

Of lamentation, like a wind, that shrills
All night in a waste land, where no one comes,
Or hath come, since the making of the world.
      Then murmured Arthur, 'Place me in the barge.'
And to the barge they came. There those three Queens
Put forth their hands, and took the King, and wept.
But she, that rose the tallest of them all
And fairest, laid his head upon her lap,
And loosed the shatter'd casque, and chafed his hands,
And call'd him by his name, complaining loud,
And dropping bitter tears against his brow
Striped with dark blood: for all his face was white
And colourless, and like the wither'd moon
Smote by the fresh beam of the springing east;
And all his greaves and cuisses dash'd with drops
Of onset; and the light and lustrous curls —
That made his forehead like a rising sun
High from the daïs-throne — were parch'd with dust;
Or, clotted into points and hanging loose,
Mix'd with the knightly growth that fringed his lips.
So like a shatter'd column lay the King;
Not like that Arthur who, with lance in rest,
From spur to plume a star of tournament,
Shot thro' the lists at Camelot, and charged
Before the eyes of ladies and of kings.
      Then loudly cried the bold Sir Bedivere,
'Ah! my Lord Arthur, whither shall I go?
Where shall I hide my forehead and my eyes?
For now I see the true old times are dead,
When every morning brought a noble chance,
And every chance brought out a noble knight.
Such times have been not since the light that led
The holy Elders with the gift of myrrh.
But now the whole ROUND TABLE is dissolved

343

Which was an image of the mighty world;
And I, the last, go forth companionless,
And the days darken round me, and the years,
Among new men, strange faces, other minds.'
 And slowly answered Arthur from the barge:
'The old order changeth, yielding place to new,
And God fulfils Himself in many ways,
Lest one good custom should corrupt the world.
Comfort thyself: what comfort is in me?
I have lived my life, and that which I have done
May He within himself make pure! but thou,
If thou shouldst never see my face again,
Pray for my soul. More things are wrought by prayer
Than this world dreams of. Wherefore, let thy voice
Rise like a fountain for me night and day.
For what are men better than sheep or goats
That nourish a blind life within the brain,
If, knowing God, they lift not hands of prayer
Both for themselves and those who call them friend?
For so the whole round earth is every way
Bound by gold chains about the feet of God.
But now farewell. I am going a long way
With these thou seëst — if indeed I go —
(For all my mind is clouded with a doubt)
To the island-valley of Avilion;
Where falls not hail, or rain, or any snow,
Nor ever wind blows loudly, but it lies
Deep-meadow'd, happy, fair with orchard lawns
And bowery hollows crown'd with summer sea,
Where I will heal me of my grievous wound.'
 So said he, and the barge with oar and sail
Moved from the brink, like some full-breasted swan
That, fluting a wild carol ere her death,
Ruffles her pure cold plume, and takes the flood

With swarthy webs. Long stood Sir Bedivere
Revolving many memories, till the hull
Look'd one black dot against the verge of dawn,
And on the mere the wailing died away.

— Alfred, Lord Tennyson

'WHATSOEVER THINGS ARE TRUE'

Whatsoever things are true,
whatsoever things are honest,
whatsoever things are just,
whatsoever things are pure,
whatsoever things are lovely,
whatsoever things are of good report;
if there be any virtue,
and if there be any praise,
think on these things.

— The Bible

*The Epistle of the Apostle Paul to the
Philippians,* IV:8

from: INSTRUCTIONS OF KING CORMAC

Be not too wise, nor too foolish,
Be not too conceited, nor diffident,
Be not too haughty, nor too humble,
Be not too talkative, nor too silent,
Be not too hard, nor too feeble.
If you be too wise, men will expect too much of you;
If you be too foolish, you will be deceived;
If you be too conceited, you will be thought vexatious;
If you be too humble, you will be without honour;
If you be too talkative, you will not be heeded;
If you be too silent, you will not be regarded;
If you be too hard, you will be broken;
If you be too feeble, you will be crushed.

— *Cormac, King of Cashel (Irish, Ninth Century)*

NO BASHFULNESSE IN BEGGING

To get thine ends, lay bashfulnesse aside;
Who fears to ask, doth teach to be denied.

— Robert Herrick

'THE CROW DOTH SING . . .'

The crow doth sing as sweetly as the lark
When neither is attended, and I think
The nightingale, if she should sing by day,
When every goose is cackling, would be thought
No better a musician than the wren.
How many things by season season'd are
To their right praise and true perfection!

— William Shakespeare

from: *The Merchant of Venice,* Act V, Scene 1

'THE QUALITY OF MERCY...'

The quality of mercy is not strain'd,
It droppeth as the gentle rain from heaven
Upon the place beneath; it is twice blest;
It blesseth him that gives and him that takes:
'Tis mightiest in the mightiest: it becomes
The throned monarch better than his crown;
His sceptre shows the force of temporal power,
The attribute to awe and majesty,
Wherein doth sit the dread and fear of kings;
But mercy is above this sceptred sway;
It is enthroned in the hearts of kings,
It is an attribute to God himself;
And earthly power doth then show likest God's
When mercy seasons justice. . . .

— *William Shakespeare*

from: *The Merchant of Venice*, Act IV, Scene 1

348

'BE NOT AFRAID . . .'

Be not afraid because the sun goes down;
It brings the sunset and the plover's cry.
Before the colors of the evening drown,
The stars will make new colors in the sky.
Night is no enemy. She passes by,
And shows us silence for our own heart's good;
For while we sleep, the roses multiply,
The little tree grows taller in the wood.
   Fear not the night; the morning follows soon.
   Each has his task to make the earth more fair.
   It is by these, by midnight and by noon,
   That she grows riper and her orchards bear.
   Her fields would wither in a sun too bright;
   They need the darkness too. Fear not the night.

— Robert Nathan

THE LITTLE DANCERS: A LONDON VISION

Lonely, save for a few faint stars, the sky
Dreams; and lonely, below, the little street
Into its gloom retires, secluded and shy.
Scarcely the dumb roar enters this soft retreat;
And all is dark, save where the flooding rays
From a tavern window: there, to the brisk measure
Of an organ that down in an alley merrily plays,
Two children, all alone and no one by,
Holding their tatter'd frocks, through an airy maze
Of motion, lightly threaded with nimble feet,
Dance sedately: face to face they gaze,
Their eyes shining, grave with a perfect pleasure.

— *Laurence Binyon*

FROLIC

The children were shouting together
  And racing along the sands,
A glimmer of dancing shadows,
  A dove-like flutter of hands.

The stars were shouting in heaven,
  The sun was chasing the moon:
The game was the same as the children's,
  They danced to the self-same tune.

The whole of the world was merry,
  One joy from the vale to the height,
Where the blue woods of twilight encircled
  The lovely lawns of the light.

— A. E. (George Russell)

EVENING AT THE FARM

Over the hill the farm-boy goes.
His shadow lengthens along the land,
A giant staff in a giant hand;
In the poplar-tree, above the spring,
The katydid begins to sing;
      The early dews are falling; —
Into the stone-heap darts the mink;
The swallows skim the river's brink;
And home to the woodland fly the crows,
When over the hill the farm-boy goes,
    Cheerily calling,
  'Co', boss! co', boss! co'! co'! co'!'
Farther, farther, over the hill,
Faintly calling, calling still,
  'Co', boss! co', boss! co'! co'!'

Into the yard the farmer goes,
With grateful heart, at the close of day:
Harness and chain are hung away;
In the wagon-shed stand yoke and plow;
The straw's in the stack, the hay in the mow.
      The cooling dews are falling; —
The friendly sheep his welcome bleat,
The pigs come grunting to his feet,
The whinnying mare her master knows,
When into the yard the farmer goes,
    His cattle calling, —
  'Co', boss! co', boss! co'! co'! co'!'
While still the cow-boy, far away,
Goes seeking those that have gone astray, —
  'Co', boss! co', boss! co'! co'!'

Now to her task the milkmaid goes.
The cattle come crowding through the gate,
Lowing, pushing, little and great;
About the trough, by the farm-yard pump,
The frolicsome yearlings frisk and jump,
     While the pleasant dews are falling; —
The new milch heifer is quick and shy,
But the old cow waits with tranquil eye,
And the white stream into the bright pail flows,
When to her task the milkmaid goes,
     Soothingly calling,
  'So, boss! so, boss! so! so! so!'
The cheerful milkmaid takes her stool,
And sits and milks in the twilight cool,
     Saying, 'So! so, boss! so! so!'

To supper at last the farmer goes.
The apples are pared, the paper read,
The stories are told, then all to bed.
Without, the crickets' ceaseless song
Makes shrill the silence all night long.
     The heavy dews are falling.
The housewife's hand has turned the lock;
Drowsily ticks the kitchen clock;
The household sinks to deep repose,
But still in sleep the farm-boy goes,
     Singing, calling, —
  'Co', boss! co', boss! co'! co'! co'!'
And oft the milkmaid, in her dreams,
Drums in the pail with the flashing streams,
     Murmuring, 'So, boss! so!'

                              — *John T. Trowbridge*

♪ from: EVENING QUATRAINS

The day's grown old; the fainting sun
Has but a little way to run:
And yet his steeds, with all his skill,
Scarce lug the chariot down the hill.

The shadows now so long do grow,
That brambles like tall cedars show;
Molehills seem mountains, and the ant
Appears a monstrous elephant.

A very little, little flock
Shades thrice the ground that it would stock;
Whilst the small stripling following them
Appears a mighty Polypheme . . .

The hedge is stript, the clothes brought in;
Naught's left without should be within.
The bees are hived, and hum their charm;
Whilst every house does seem a swarm.

— Charles Cotton

EVENSONG

The embers of the day are red
Beyond the murky hill.
The kitchen smokes: the bed
In the darkling house is spread:
The great sky darkens overhead,
And the great woods are shrill.
So far have I been led,

Lord, by Thy will:
So far I have followed, Lord, and wondered still.

The breeze from the embalmèd land
Blows sudden toward the shore,
And claps my cottage door.
I hear the signal, Lord — I understand.
The night at Thy command
Comes. I will eat and sleep and will not question more.

— *Robert Louis Stevenson*

GOOD HOURS

I had for my winter evening walk —
No one at all with whom to talk,
But I had the cottages in a row
Up to their shining eyes in snow.

And I thought I had the folk within:
I had the sound of a violin;
I had a glimpse through curtain laces
Of youthful forms and youthful faces.

I had such company outward bound.
I went till there were no cottages found.
I turned and repeated, but coming back
I saw no window but that was black.

Over the snow my creaking feet
Disturbed the slumbering village street
Like profanation, by your leave,
At ten o'clock of a winter eve.

— *Robert Frost*

STARS

Now in the West the slender moon lies low,
And now Orion glimmers through the trees,
Clearing the earth with even pace and slow,
And now the stately-moving Pleiades,
In that soft infinite darkness overhead
Hang jewel-wise upon a silver thread.

And all the lonelier stars that have their place,
Calm lamps within the distant southern sky,
And planet-dust upon the edge of space,
Look down upon the fretful world, and I
Look up to outer vastness unafraid
And see the stars which sang when earth was made.

— Marjorie Pickthall

NIGHT-PIECE

Her eyes the glow-worm lend thee,
The shooting stars attend thee:
    And the elves also,
    Whose little eyes glow,
Like the sparks of fire, befriend thee.

No will-o'-the-wisp mis-light thee;
Nor snake or slow-worm bite thee:
    But on, on thy way
    Not making a stay,
Since ghost there's none to fright thee.

Let not the dark thee cumber;
What though the moon does slumber?
  The stars of the night
  Will lend thee their light,
Like tapers without number.

— Robert Herrick

THE MOON

Thy beauty haunts me heart and soul,
  Oh thou fair Moon, so close and bright;
Thy beauty makes me like the child,
  That cries aloud to own thy light:
The little child that lifts each arm,
To press thee to her bosom warm.

Though there are birds that sing this night
  With thy white beams across their throats,
Let my deep silence speak for me
  More than for them their sweetest notes:
Who worships thee till music fails
Is greater than thy nightingales.

— W. H. Davies

SILVER

Slowly, silently, now the moon
Walks the night in her silver shoon;
This way, and that, she peers, and sees
Silver fruit upon silver trees;
One by one the casements catch
Her beams beneath the silvery thatch;
Couched in his kennel, like a log,
With paws of silver sleeps the dog;
From their shadowy cote the white breasts peep
Of doves in a silver-feathered sleep;
A harvest mouse goes scampering by,
With silver claws and silver eye;
And moveless fish in the water gleam,
By silver reeds in a silver stream.

— *Walter de la Mare*

MOONLIT APPLES

At the top of the house the apples are laid in rows,
And the skylight lets the moonlight in, and those
Apples are deep-sea apples of green. There goes
  A cloud on the moon in the autumn night.

A mouse in the wainscot scratches, and scratches, and then
There is no sound at the top of the house of men
Or mice; and the cloud is blown, and the moon again
  Dapples the apples with deep-sea light.

They are lying in rows there, under the gloomy beams;
On the sagging floor; they gather the silver streams

Out of the moon, those moonlit apples of dreams,
   And quiet is the steep stair under.

In the corridors under there is nothing but sleep,
And stiller than ever on orchard boughs they keep
Tryst with the moon, and deep is the silence, deep
   On moon-washed apples of wonder.

                              — *John Drinkwater*

FULL MOON

One night as Dick lay half asleep,
      Into his drowsy eyes
A great still light began to creep
      From out the silent skies.
It was the lovely moon's, for when
      He raised his dreamy head,
Her surge of silver filled the pane
      And streamed across his bed.
So, for a while, each gazed at each —
      Dick and the solemn moon —
Till, climbing slowly on her way,
      She vanished, and was gone.

                              — *Walter de la Mare*

WASHED IN SILVER

Gleaming in silver are the hills!
Blazing in silver is the sea!

And a silvery radiance spills
Where the moon drives royally!

Clad in silver tissue, I
March magnificently by!

— James Stephens

I SEE THE MOON

I see the moon,
And the moon sees me;
God bless the moon,
And God bless me.

— Traditional: English

LAST SONG

To the Sun
Who has shone
   All day,
To the Moon
Who has gone
   Away,
To the milk-white,
Silk-white,
Lily-white Star
A fond goodnight
Wherever you are.

— James Guthrie

ON A QUIET CONSCIENCE

Close thine eyes, and sleep secure;
Thy soul is safe, thy body sure.
He that guards thee, he that keeps,
Never slumbers, never sleeps.
A quiet conscience in the breast
Has only peace, has only rest.
The wisest and the mirth of kings
Are out of tune unless she sings:
Then close thine eyes in peace and sleep secure,
No sleep so sweet as thine, no rest so sure.

— Charles I of England

♭ MATTHEW, MARK, LUKE, AND JOHN

Matthew, Mark, Luke, and John,
Bless the bed that I lie on;
Four corners to my bed,
Four angels there be spread:
One at the head, one at the feet,
And two to guard me while I sleep.
God within and God without,
And Jesus Christ all round about;
I go by sea, I go by land,
The Lord made me with His right hand.
If any danger come to me,
Sweet Jesus Christ deliver me.
He's the branch and I'm the flower,
Pray God send me a happy hour,
And if I die before I wake,
I pray that Christ my soul will take.

— Traditional: English

362

IRISH LULLABY

I'd rock my own sweet childie to rest in a cradle of gold on
    a bough of the willow,
To the *shoheen ho* of the wind of the west and the *lulla lo*
    of the soft sea billow.
          Sleep, baby dear,
          Sleep without fear,
    Mother is here beside your pillow.

I'd put my own sweet childie to sleep in a silver boat on
    the beautiful river,
Where *a shoheen* whisper the white cascades, and *a lulla lo*
    the green flags shiver.
          Sleep, baby dear,
          Sleep without fear,
    Mother is here with you for ever.

Lulla lo! to the rise and fall of mother's bosom 'tis sleep
    has bound you,
And O, my child, what cosier nest for rosier rest could love
    have found you?
          Sleep, baby dear,
          Sleep without fear,
    Mother's two arms are clasped around you.

— Alfred Perceval Graves

'SING ALL YE JOYFUL . . .'

A Lullaby for Bilbo Baggins

Sing all ye joyful, now sing all together!
The wind's in the tree-top, the wind's in the heather;
The stars are in blossom, the moon is in flower,
And bright are the windows of Night in her tower.

Dance all ye joyful, now dance all together!
Soft is the grass, and let foot be like feather!
The river is silver, the shadows are fleeting;
Merry is May-time, and merry our meeting.

Sing we now softly, and dreams let us weave him!
Wind him in slumber and there let us leave him!
The wanderer sleepeth. Now soft be his pillow!
Lullaby! Lullaby! Alder and Willow!
Sigh no more Pine, till the wind of the morn!
    Fall Moon! Dark be the land!
    Hush! Hush! Oak, Ash and Thorn!
Hushed be all water, till dawn is at hand!

— J. R. R. Tolkien

from: *The Hobbit*

WHERE

Monkeys in a forest,
Beggarmen in rags,
Marrow in a knucklebone,
Gold in leather bags;

Dumplings in the oven,
Fishes in a pool,
Flowers in the parlour,
Dunces in a school;

Feathers in a pillow,
Cattle in a shed,
Honey in a beehive,
And me in bed.

— *Walter de la Mare*

from: AN OLD CORNISH LITANY

From Ghoulies and Ghosties,
And long-leggity Beasties,
And all Things that go bump in the Night,
Good Lord deliver us.

THE BELL-MAN

From noise of scare-fires rest ye free,
From Murders — *Benedicite.*
From all mischances, that may fright
Your pleasing slumbers in the night:
Mercy secure ye all, and keep
The Goblin from ye, while ye sleep.
Past one o'clock, and almost two,
My Masters all, *Good day to you!*

— *Robert Herrick*

from: EPITHALAMIUM

Let no lamenting cries, nor doleful tears,
Be heard all night within nor yet without;
Ne let false whispers, breeding hidden fears,
Break gentle sleep with misconceived doubt.
Let no deluding dreams nor dreadful sights
Make sudden sad affrights;
Ne let housefires, nor lightning's helpless harms,
Ne let the Puck, nor other evil sprights,
Ne let mischievous witches with their charms,
Ne let hobgoblins, names whose sense we see not,
Fray us with things that be not.
Let not the screech owl, nor the stork be heard;
Nor the night raven that still deadly yells,
Nor damnèd ghosts called up with mighty spells,
Nor grisly vultures make us once affeared:
Ne let th' unpleasant quire of frogs still croaking
Make us to wish their choking.
Let none of these their dreary accents sing;
Ne let the woods them answer, nor their echo ring.

But let still silence true night watches keep,
That sacred peace may in assurance reign,
And timely sleep, when it is time to sleep,
May pour his limbs forth on your pleasant plain,
The whiles an hundred little wingèd loves
Like divers feathered doves,
Shall fly and flutter round about your bed.

— Edmund Spenser

THE NIGHT WILL NEVER STAY

The night will never stay,
The night will still go by,
Though with a million stars
You pin it to the sky;
Though you bind it with the blowing wind
And buckle it with the moon,
The night will slip away
Like sorrow or a tune.

— Eleanor Farjeon

THEN

Twenty, forty, sixty, eighty,
  A hundred years ago,
All through the night with lantern bright
  The Watch trudged to and fro.
And little boys tucked snug abed
  Would wake from dreams to hear —
'Two o' the morning by the clock,
  And the stars a-shining clear!'
Or, when across the chimney-tops
  Screamed shrill a North-east gale,
A faint and shaken voice would shout,
  'Three! and a storm of hail!'

— Walter de la Mare

𝄞 SONG OF THE WATCHMEN

Past three o'clock,
And a cold frosty morning:
Past three o'clock,
Good morrow masters all.
While in your beds you're peacefully sleeping,
Under the stars our watch we are keeping.
Past three o'clock,
And a cold frosty morning,
Past three o'clock,
Good morrow masters all.

We go the rounds, you rest at your leisure,
Safe is your house and safe is your treasure,
Past three o'clock,
And a cold frosty morning,
Past three o'clock,
Good morrow masters all.

When morning breaks, and slumber is ended,
Give us your thanks, your homes who've defended;
Past three o'clock,
And a cold frosty morning,
Past three o'clock,
Good morrow masters all.

— Attributed to *James Fortescue*

THE DAWN WIND

At two o'clock in the morning, if you open your window
    and listen,
You will hear the feet of the Wind that is going to call the
    sun.
And the trees in the shadow rustle and the trees in the
    moonlight glisten,
And though it is deep, dark night, you feel that the night
    is done.

So do the cows in the field. They graze for an hour and lie
    down,
Dozing and chewing the cud; or a bird in the ivy wakes,
Chirrups one note and is still, and the restless Wind strays
    on,
Fidgeting far down the road, till, softly, the darkness breaks.

Back comes the Wind full strength, with a blow like an
    angel's wing,
Gentle but waking the world, as he shouts: 'The sun! The
    Sun!'
And the light floods over the fields and the birds begin to
    sing,
And the wind dies down in the grass. It is Day and his
    work is done.

So when the world is asleep, and there seems no hope of
    her waking
Out of the long, bad dream that makes her mutter and
    moan
Suddenly all men rise to the noise of fetters breaking,
And everyone smiles at his neighbour and tells him his soul
    is his own.

                — *Rudyard Kipling*

♪ PACK, CLOUDS, AWAY

Pack, clouds, away, and welcome, day!
With night we banish sorrow.
Sweet air, blow soft; mount, lark, aloft
To give my love good morrow.
Wings from the wind to please her mind,
Notes from the lark I'll borrow:
Bird, prune thy wing, nightingale, sing,
To give my love good morrow;
    To give my love good morrow,
      Notes from them all I'll borrow.

Wake from thy nest, robin redbreast!
Sing, birds, in every furrow,
And from each bill let music shrill
Give my fair love good morrow.
Black-bird and thrush in every bush,
Stare, linnet and cock-sparrow,
You pretty elves, amongst yourselves
Sing my fair love good morrow.
    To give my love good morrow,
      Sing, birds, in every furrow.

             — *Thomas Heywood*

REVEILLE

Wake: the silver dusk returning
  Up the beach of darkness brims,
And the ship of sunrise burning
  Strands upon the eastern rims.

Wake: the vaulted shadow shatters,
  Trampled to the floor it spanned,
And the tent of night in tatters
  Straws the sky-pavilioned land.

Up, lad, up, 'tis late for lying:
  Hear the drums of morning play;
Hark, the empty highways crying
  'Who'll beyond the hills away?'

Towns and countries woo together,
  Forelands beacon, belfries call;
Never lad that trod on leather
  Lived to feast his heart with all.

Up, lad: thews that lie and cumber
  Sunlit pallets never thrive;
Morns abed and daylight slumber
  Were not meant for man alive.

Clay lies still, but blood's a rover;
  Breath's a ware that will not keep.
Up, lad: when the journey's over
  There'll be time enough to sleep.

— A. E. Housman

'YONDER SEE THE MORNING BLINK'

Yonder see the morning blink:
 The sun is up, and up must I,
To wash and dress and eat and drink
And look at things and talk and think
 And work, and God knows why.

Oh often have I washed and dressed
 And what's to show for all my pain?
Let me lie abed and rest:
Ten thousand times I've done my best
 And all's to do again.

      — A. E. Housman

BEAUTY

Beauty is seen
In the sunlight,
The trees, the birds,
Corn growing and people working
Or dancing for their harvest.

Beauty is heard
In the night,
Wind sighing, rain falling,
Or a singer chanting
Anything in earnest.

Beauty is in yourself.
Good deeds, happy thoughts
That repeat themselves
In your dreams,
In your work,
And even in your rest.

— E-Yeh-Shure

THE UNCHARTED

The boundaries of heaven may be
Less wide than night's immensity,
Less high than snowy peak or spire.
A lamplit pane, a kindled fire,
A room, an acre, or a mile,
Or the brief space it takes a smile
To cross the threshold of a heart —
These no cartographer may chart,
Or instrument have power to give
The latitudes by which we live.

— *Rachel Field*

DREAMS

Hold fast to dreams
For if dreams die
Life is a broken-winged bird
That cannot fly.

Hold fast to dreams
For when dreams go
Life is a barren field
Frozen with snow.

— *Langston Hughes*

♪ SONG

Tell me where is fancy bred,
Or in the heart or in the head?
How begot, how nourished?
    Reply, reply.
    It is engendered in the eyes,
    With gazing fed; and fancy dies
In the cradle where it lies.
    Let us all ring fancy's knell:
    I'll begin it, — Ding, dong, bell.

— *William Shakespeare*

from: *The Merchant of Venice,* Act III, Scene 2

'WHAT IS ONCE LOVED'

What is once loved
You will find
Is always yours
From that day.
Take it home
In your mind
And nothing ever
Can take it away.

— *Elizabeth Coatsworth*

from: The GREAT LOVER

These I have loved:
        White plates and cups, clean-gleaming,
Ringed with blue lines; and feathery, faery dust;
Wet roofs, beneath the lamp-light; the strong crust
Of friendly bread; and many-tasting food;
Rainbows; and the blue bitter smoke of wood;
And radiant raindrops couching in cool flowers;
And flowers themselves, that sway through sunny hours,
Dreaming of moths that drink them under the moon;
Then, the cool kindliness of sheets, that soon
Smooth away trouble; and the rough male kiss
Of blankets; grainy wood; live hair that is
Shining and free; blue-massing clouds; the keen
Unpassioned beauty of a great machine;
The benison of hot water; furs to touch;
The good smell of old clothes; and other such —
The comfortable smell of friendly fingers,
Hair's fragrance, and the musty reek that lingers
About dead leaves and last year's ferns. . . .
                    Dear names,
And thousand other throng to me! Royal flames;
Sweet water's dimpling laugh from tap or spring;
Holes in the ground; and voices that do sing;
Voices in laughter, too; and body's pain,
Soon turned to peace; and the deep-panting train;
Firm sands; the little dulling edge of foam
That browns and dwindles as the wave goes home;
And washen stones, gay for an hour; the cold
Graveness of iron; moist black earthen mould;

Sleep; and high places; footprints in the dew;
And oaks; and brown horse-chestnuts, glossy-new;
And new-peeled sticks; and shining pools on grass; —
All these have been my loves.

— Rupert Brooke

♪ I LOVE ALL BEAUTEOUS THINGS

I love all beauteous things,
  I seek and adore them;
God hath no better praise,
And man in his hasty days
  Is honoured for them.

I too will something make
  And joy in the making;
Altho' tomorrow it seem
Like the empty words of a dream
  Remembered on waking.

— Robert Bridges

THE GLASS-BLOWER

By the red furnace stands
  Apollo mute,
Holding in upraised hands
  His iron flute.
Slowly from back and brow
  The bright sweat drips;
He sets the clarion now
  Light to his lips,

And ever, as he blows,
   Without a sound
His molten music flows,
   Golden and round.

Never from herald's breath
   In brazen horn,
Telling of strife and death
   Or of peace new-born;
From silver clarinet
   By fingers small
To lips of ruby set
   In raftered hall;
From jilted shepherd's reed
   Plaintively proving
How he in very deed
   Must die of loving —
Never from all these came
   A music sweeter
Than this bright sphere of flame
With neither sound nor name,
   Cadence nor metre,
That steadily, as he blows
   On his iron flute,
Trembles and swells and glows,
Gold-amber, amber-rose.
   In melody mute.

— Jan Struther

'BRIGHT IS THE RING OF WORDS'

Bright is the ring of words
   When the right man rings them,
Fair the fall of songs
   When the singer sings them.
Still they are carolled and said —
   On wings they are carried —
After the singer is dead
   And the maker buried.

— Robert Louis Stevenson

ON FIRST LOOKING INTO CHAPMAN'S HOMER

Much have I travelled in the realms of gold,
And many goodly states and kingdoms seen;
Round many western islands have I been
Which bards in fealty to Apollo hold.
Oft of one wide expanse had I been told
That deep-browed Homer ruled as his demesne;
Yet did I never breathe its pure serene
Till I heard Chapman speak out loud and bold:
Then felt I like some watcher of the skies
When a new planet swims into his ken;
Or like stout Cortes when with eagle eyes
He stared at the Pacific, — and all his men
Looked at each other with a wild surmise, —
Silent, upon a peak in Darien.

— John Keats

SALUTE TO THE MANTUAN

O gouden was the Whinnie Brae
I wandered as a bairn,
But I sawna the gowan there,
I sawna the fern.
The ae leaf I gliskit
In the mornins dule
Was in the wee Latin buik
The hale mile to schule.

And daunderin' doon the brae hame
Wi' Vergil in my loof
Troy warked sae greatly in my wame,
Tae pit it tae the proof
I wad hae made a wudden horse
Oot o' ilk aiken tree,
And cut the rowans intae spears
For sake o' chivalrie.

— *Lewis Spence*

PARAPHRASE

O golden was the Whinnie Brae
I wandered as a child,
But I saw not the daisy there,
I saw not the fern.
The only leaf I noticed
In the morning's dusk
Was in the wee Latin book
The whole mile to school.

And sauntering down the hill home
With Vergil in my hand
Troy worked so greatly in my imagination
To put it to the proof
I would have made a wooden horse
Out of each oak tree,
And cut the rowans into spears
For sake of chivalry.

EVERYONE SANG

1917

Everyone suddenly burst out singing;
And I was filled with such delight
As prisoned birds must find in freedom,
Winging wildly across the white
Orchards and dark green fields; on — on — and out of sight.

Everyone's voice was suddenly lifted,
And beauty came like the setting sun.
My heart was shaken with tears, and horror
Drifted away . . . O, but Everyone
Was a bird; and the song was wordless; the singing will
    never be done.

— Siegfried Sassoon

EGYPT'S MIGHT IS TUMBLED DOWN

Egypt's might is tumbled down,
   Down a-down the deeps of thought;
Greece is fallen and Troy town,
Glorious Rome hath lost her crown,
   Venice' pride is naught.

But the dreams their children dreamed,
   Fleeting, unsubstantial, vain,
Shadowy as the shadows seemed,
Airy nothings, as they deemed —
   These remain.

— Mary E. Coleridge

'OUR REVELS NOW ARE ENDED ...'

Our revels now are ended. These our actors,
As I foretold you, were all spirits and
Are melted into air, into thin air:
And, like the baseless fabric of this vision,
The cloud-capp'd towers, the gorgeous palaces,
The solemn temples, the great globe itself,
Yea, all which it inherit, shall dissolve
And, like this insubstantial pageant faded,
Leave not a rack behind. We are such stuff
As dreams are made on, and our little life
Is rounded with a sleep.

— William Shakespeare

from: *The Tempest*, Act IV, Scene 1

Who would true valour see,
Let him come hither;
One here will constant be,
Come wind, come weather;
There's no discouragement,
Shall make him once relent,
His first avow'd intent,
To be a pilgrim.

Whoso beset him round,
With dismal stories,
Do but themselves confound;
His strength the more is.
No lion can him fright
He'll with a giant fight,
But he will have a right,
To be a pilgrim.

Hobgoblin, nor foul fiend,
Can daunt his spirit:
He knows, he at the end,
Shall Life inherit.
Then fancies fly away,
He'll fear not what men say,
He'll labour night and day,
To be a pilgrim.

— *John Bunyan*

from: *The Pilgrim's Progress*, Part II

TO THE CHILDREN

Do you remember the old song?
'This is the way he sows the seed,
So early in the morning.'

This is your world, your broad and furrowed fields,
Here what you plough will bear its fruit in time.
This friendly loam a richer garden yields
Than there, where the untended thistles climb.
Here are the roses for your hours of grace,
And there the stones to keep your meadows neat;
You shall declare the future of this place,
What shall be stone, what shall be flower and wheat —
What shall be love tomorrow when the spring
Returns across this winter and this land,
Bringing the dogwood and the robin's wing,
Bearing your own sweet summer in her hand.
That this may grow and ripen to your need,
Now mark the furrow well, and sow the seed.

'This is the way he sows the seed,
Sows the seed, sows the seed,
This is the way he sows the seed,
So early in the morning.'

— *Robert Nathan*

ACKNOWLEDGMENTS

TO the following publishers, authors and literary trustees whose generosity in the matter of copyright has made this collection possible, the editors make grateful acknowledgment:

To George E. Abbot, Trustee u/w Laura E. Richards, for "Old Ducky Quackerel."

To George Allen & Unwin Ltd., for "Roads go ever on," five riddles, and "Sing all ye joyful" from *The Hobbit* by J. R. R. Tolkien, published by George Allen & Unwin Ltd.

To The American Museum of Natural History, for "Prayer to the Dark Bird" from *The Night Chant, A Navaho Ceremony* printed in the Memoir Series of the American Museum.

To Martin Armstrong for his poem "Mrs. Reece Laughs."

To Violet Barton, acting for Walter de la Mare and Faber & Faber Ltd., for "Eeka, Neeka," "The Old Tailor," "The Prince," "The Snowflake," and "Where" from *Bells and Grass*; for "Farewell," "I Saw Three Witches," and "The Hare" from *Collected Poems*; for "Berries," "Full Moon," "Silver," "The Cupboard," and "Then" from *Peacock Pie*; and for "The Fiddlers" from *Rhymes and Verses,* all by Walter de la Mare.

To Ernest Benn Ltd., for "The Blackbird" and "The Lilac" from *Kensington Gardens* by Humbert Wolfe.

To Basil Blackwell & Mott, Ltd., Oxford, for "Goblin Feet" by J. R. R. Tolkien and for "The Little Ships" from *The Second Lustre* by Hilton Brown. By permission of Basil Blackwell & Mott, Ltd., Oxford.

To William Blackwood & Sons, Ltd., for "Grace for Light" from *Songs of the Glens of Antrim,* by permission of Moira O'Neill, and for "A Song of Sherwood" from *The Collected Poems* of Alfred Noyes, both published by William Blackwood & Sons, Ltd.

To Brandt & Brandt, for "A Counting-Out Rhyme" from *The Buck in the Snow and Other Poems,* published by Harper & Brothers, Copyright, 1928, by Edna St. Vincent Millay; for "God's World" from *Renascence and Other Poems,* published by Harper & Brothers, Copyright, 1917, by Edna St. Vincent Millay; for "Nancy Hanks" from *A Book of Americans,* published by Rinehart & Co., Inc., Copyright, 1933, by Rosemary Carr Benét; and for "The Ballad of William Sycamore" from *Selected Works of Stephen Vincent Benét,* published by Rinehart & Co., Inc., Copyright, 1922, by Stephen Vincent Benét.

To Brown, Son & Ferguson, Ltd., for "The Whale" by W. H. Whall from *Sea Songs and Shanties* published by Brown, Son & Ferguson, Ltd., 52-58 Darnley Street, Glasgow.

To Burns Oates & Washbourne Ltd., for "The Rainy Summer" by Alice Meynell and "To a Snowflake" by Francis Thompson.

To S. D. Campbell, for "I Will Go with My Father A-Ploughing" by Joseph Campbell.

To Jonathan Cape Ltd., for "Hill Pastures" from *A Mary Webb Anthology,* Selected and Edited by H. B. L. Webb, by permission of The Trustees of the Mary Webb Estate and Jonathan Cape Ltd., publishers; also for "A Great Time" and "The Moon" from *The Collected Poems of W. H. Davies,* by permission of the Trustees of the W. H. Davies Estate and Jonathan Cape Ltd., publishers.

To The Clarendon Press, for "I Love All Beauteous Things" and "London Snow" from *Shorter Poems* by Robert Bridges (Clarendon Press, Oxford).

Acknowledgments

To Padraic Colum, for ¨An Old Woman of the Roads" from *Poems*, published by The Macmillan Co., New York, and Macmillan & Co., Ltd., London.

To Constable & Co., Ltd., for "Saint Patrick's Breastplate," printed under the title of "The Deer's Cry" in *Selections from Ancient Irish Poetry* by Kuno Meyer, published by Constable & Co., Ltd., London.

To Frances Cornford, for her poem "To a Fat Lady Seen from the Train," through the courtesy of the Poetry Bookshop.

To Coward-McCann, Inc., for "The Mouse," reprinted from *Compass Rose* by Elizabeth Coatsworth, copyright, 1929, by Coward-McCann, Inc.

To Curtis Brown, Ltd., London, for Ogden Nash's poem "A Carol for Children" from *The Face is Familiar*, included by permission of the author and J. M. Dent & Sons Limited; for "A Wish" from *Come Christmas* by Eleanor Farjeon, by permission of the author; for "Carol" and "Ducks' Ditty" by Kenneth Grahame, through the courtesy of Messrs. Methuen & Co. Ltd. and Mrs. Kenneth Grahame; for "Moonlit Apples" by John Drinkwater, included in *Poems of Today* published by Messrs. Sidgwick & Jackson, by permission of the author's executors and Messrs. Sidgwick & Jackson Ltd.; for "The Ending of the Year" and "The Shepherd and the King" by Eleanor Farjeon, included by permission of the author; for "We Who Were Born" from *Dew on the Grass* and for "Winter's End" from *Morning Songs and Other Poems*, both by Eiluned Lewis.

To Curtis Brown, Ltd., New York, for "Moonlit Apples" by John Drinkwater, Copyright, 1919, by John Drinkwater. Reprinted by permission of the author's estate; and for "The Glass-Blower" and "To an Orchard Near London" from *The Glass-Blower and Other Poems*, copyright, 1941, by Jan Struther. Reprinted by permission of the author.

To J. M. Dent & Sons Ltd., for "I Stood Tip-Toe Upon a Little Hill" from the Everyman's Library edition of John Keats's *Poems* and for "The Canticle of the Sun" of St. Francis of Assisi adapted from the translation of Robert Steele, from Everyman's Library, published by J. M. Dent & Sons Ltd.

To Dodd, Mead and Company for "An Almanac" and "The Field Mouse" from *Poems* by William Sharp. Reprinted by permission of DODD, MEAD & COMPANY; for "Song of the Dog 'Quoodle'" from *The Flying Inn* by G. K. Chesterton. Copyright, 1914, by Dodd, Mead & Company. Reprinted by permission of DODD, MEAD & COMPANY; and for an excerpt from "The Great Lover" from *Collected Poems of Rupert Brooke*, copyright, 1915, by Dodd, Mead and Company. Reprinted by permission of DODD, MEAD & COMPANY.

To Doubleday & Company, Inc., for "Big Steamers" and "The Dawn Wind" by Rudyard Kipling from: *A History of England* by C. R. L. Fletcher and Rudyard Kipling, copyright, 1911, by Rudyard Kipling, reprinted by permission of Mrs. George Bambridge and Doubleday & Company, Inc.; for "Miracles" from *Leaves of Grass* by Walt Whitman, copyright, 1924, by Doubleday & Company, Inc.; for "Road-Song of the Bandar Log" and "Seal Lullaby" from *The Jungle Book* by Rudyard Kipling, copyright, 1893, 1894, 1932, courtesy of Doubleday & Co., Inc.; for "The Blackbird" and "The Lilac" from *Kensington Gardens* by Humbert Wolfe, reprinted by permission of Doubleday & Company, Inc.

To Gerald Duckworth & Co., Ltd., for "The Frog" from *Bad Child's Book of Beasts* by Hilaire Belloc, published by Gerald Duckworth & Co., Ltd., and for "The Gnu" from *A Moral Alphabet* by Hilaire Belloc, published by Gerald Duckworth & Co., Ltd.

To E. P. Dutton & Co., Inc., for "A Soft Day" taken from *Songs from Leinster* by Winifred M. Letts, published by E. P. Dutton & Co., Inc., New York; for "Hill Pastures" taken from *A Mary Webb Anthology*, Selected and Edited by H. B. L. Webb,

Acknowledgments

published and copyright by E. P. Dutton & Co., Inc., New York, 1940; for "I Stood Tip-Toe Upon a Little Hill" from Everyman's Library edition of John Keats's *Poems,* published in the United States by E. P. Dutton & Co., Inc., New York; and for "The Canticle of the Sun" of St. Francis of Assisi, adapted from the translation of Robert Steele, published in the Everyman's Library in the United States by E. P. Dutton & Co., Inc., New York.

To Faber & Faber Ltd., for "On a Cat, Ageing" from *Gossip* by Alexander Gray, for "Salute to the Mantuan" from *Weirds and Vanities* by Lewis Spence, and for "The Fourth Shepherd" from *The Cortege* by Alexander McKenzie Davidson, all three volumes published by Faber & Faber Ltd.

To Eleanor Farjeon for her poems "For a Mocking Voice," "The Children's Bells," and "The Night Will Never Stay" from *Collection of Poems* by Eleanor Farjeon published by W. Collins Sons & Co., Ltd.

To Arthur Geddes for "Irish Lullaby" by Alfred P. Graves.

To G. Rostrevor Hamilton for his poem "Tugs."

To the Reverend William H. Hamilton, D.D., for his poem "Hymn for Harvest-Time" from *Holyrood, Scottish Anthology of 1929,* published by J. M. Dent & Sons Ltd.

To Harcourt, Brace and Company for "Prayer for this House" from *This Singing World* edited by Louis Untermeyer, copyright, 1923, by Harcourt, Brace and Company, Inc., and for "The Glass-Blower" and "To an Orchard Near London" from *The Glass-Blower and Other Poems,* copyright, 1941, by Jan Struther. Reprinted by permission of Harcourt, Brace and Company, Inc.

To Henry Harrison for "Missouri" by Caroline Lawrence Dier.

To Sally Harrison, acting for Hazel Fetzer, for "The Dick Johnson Reel" reprinted from *The Bulls of Spring: Selected Poems of Jake Falstaff.* G. P. Putnam's Sons, New York. (c) Hazel Fetzer.

To F. W. Harvey for his poem "Ducks."

To William Heinemann, Ltd., for "The Seed Shop" from *Poems* by Muriel Stuart, published by William Heinemann, Ltd.

To Henry Holt and Company for "Farewell," "I Saw Three Witches," and "The Hare" from *Collected Poems* by Walter de la Mare. Copyright, 1920, by Henry Holt and Company; for "Berries," "Full Moon," "Silver," "The Cupboard," and "Then" from *Peacock Pie* by Walter de la Mare; for "The Fiddlers" from *Rhymes and Verses* by Walter de la Mare. Copyright, 1947, by Henry Holt and Company, Inc.; for "The Little Spring Flows Clear Again" from *Collected Poems* by Glenn Ward Dresbach; for "Gathering Leaves," "Good Hours," "Mending Wall," "The Last Word of a Bluebird," "The Runaway," and "The Tuft of Flowers" from *Collected Poems of Robert Frost;* for "Loveliest of Trees," "Reveille," and "The Night is Freezing Fast" from *A Shropshire Lad* (Authorized Edition) by A. E. Housman; for "Yonder See the Morning Blink" from *Last Poems* by A. E. Housman; and for "Lost" from *Chicago Poems* by Carl Sandburg, all aforementioned volumes published by Henry Holt and Company.

To Houghton Mifflin Company for "Charm for Going A-Hunting," "Homesickness," "San Francisco," "The Brown Bear," and "Western Magic" from *The Children Sing in the Far West* by Mary Austin; for "Roads Go Ever On," and "Sing All Ye Joyful" from *The Hobbit* by J. R. R. Tolkien, both volumes published by Houghton Mifflin Company.

To Alfred A. Knopf, Inc., for "A Farmer Remembers Lincoln" reprinted from *Grenstone Poems* by Witter Bynner, by permission of Alfred A. Knopf, Inc. Copyright, 1917, 1926, by Alfred A. Knopf, Inc., for "A Page's Road Song" reprinted from *The Collected Poems of William Alexander Percy* by permission of Alfred A. Knopf, Inc. Copyright, 1915, 1943, by LeRoy Pratt Percy; for "Be Not Afraid" and "To The

Acknowledgments

Children" reprinted from *A Winter Tide* by Robert Nathan, by permission of Alfred A. Knopf, Inc. Copyright, 1940, by Robert Nathan; for "Dreams" and "Mother to Son" reprinted from *The Dream Keeper* by Langston Hughes, by permission of Alfred A. Knopf, Inc. Copyright, 1932, by Alfred A. Knopf, Inc.; for "The Gnu" and "The Frog" reprinted from *Cautionary Verses* by Hilaire Belloc, by permission of Alfred A. Knopf, Inc. Copyright, 1931, by Hilaire Belloc; for "The Fiddling Lad" reprinted from *Verse* by Adelaide Crapsey, by permission of Alfred A. Knopf, Inc. Copyright, 1922, by Algernon S. Crapsey, 1934, by Adelaide T. Crapsey; and for "The Old Ships" from *The Collected Poems of James Elroy Flecker.*

To J. B. Lippincott Company for "A Wish," "The Ending of the Year," and "The Shepherd and the King" reprinted by permission of the publishers from *Come Christmas* by Eleanor Farjeon. Copyright, 1927, by J. B. Lippincott Company; for "Forty Singing Seamen," and "A Song of Sherwood" reprinted by permission of the publishers, J. B. Lippincott Company, from *Collected Poems in One Volume* by Alfred Noyes. Copyright, 1906, by Alfred Noyes; for "Little Dame Crump" reprinted by permission from *Four and Twenty Blackbirds, Nursery Rhymes of Yesterday Recalled for Children of Today,* collected by Helen Dean Fish. Copyright, 1937, by J. B. Lippincott Company.

To Little, Brown & Company for "Little John Bottlejohn" from *Tirra Lirra* by Laura E. Richards; for "The Lonely House" and "Sunrise and Sunset" from *The Poems of Emily Dickinson* edited by Martha Dickinson Bianchi and Alfred Leete Hampson; for "A Carol for Children" from *The Face is Familiar* by Ogden Nash. Copyright, 1936, by Ogden Nash. Reprinted by permission of Little, Brown and Company.

To Joan Mackenzie for her poem "The Stolen Princess."

To Hamish Maclaren for his poem "Carol."

To The Macmillan Company for "Abraham Lincoln Walks at Midnight" from *The Congo and Other Poems* by Vachel Lindsay; for "Afterwards" and "Weathers" from *Collected Poems* by Thomas Hardy; for "April Showers," "Breakfast Time," "Little Things," "Seamus Beg," "The Cherry Tree," "The Fifteen Acres," "The Rivals," "The Voice of God," "Washed in Silver," and "White Fields" from *Collected Poems* by James Stephens; for "Cargoes" from *Poems* by John Masefield; for "Frolic" from *Collected Poems* by A. E.; for "Aedh Wishes for the Cloths of Heaven," "The Lake Isle of Innisfree," and "The Song of the Wandering Aengus" from *Collected Poems* by W. B. Yeats; for "Labor of Field" and "The Salt Hay" from *Country Poems* by Elizabeth Coatsworth; for "Late October" from *Collected Poems* by Sara Teasdale; for "Spring Quiet" and "The Months" from *Poetical Works* by Christina Rossetti; for "Square-Toed Princes" from *Collected Poems* by R. P. T. Coffin; for "Two Women Under a Maple" from *There Will Be Bread and Love* by R. P. T. Coffin; for excerpt from "Sylvie and Bruno" from *Collected Verses* by Lewis Carroll; for "The Little Dancers: A London Vision" from *Collected Poems* by Laurence Binyon; for "Violet Daffodils" from *The Littlest House* by Elizabeth Coatsworth; for "What is Once Loved" from *Alice All By Herself* by Elizabeth Coatsworth; for "We Who Were Born" from *Dew on the Grass* by Eiluned Lewis; and for "Worlds" from *Collected Poems* by W. W. Gibson, all by permission of The Macmillan Company, publishers.

To The Macmillan Company of Canada for "Big Steamers" and "The Dawn Wind" by Rudyard Kipling from *A History of England* by C. R. L. Fletcher and Rudyard Kipling, and for "Road-Song of the Bandar Log" and "Seal Lullaby" from *The Jungle Book* by Rudyard Kipling.

To Macmillan & Co. Ltd. and the Trustees of the Hardy Estate for "Afterwards"

Acknowledgments

and "Weathers" from *Collected Poems* by Thomas Hardy; for "Frolic" taken from *Collected Poems* by A. E., by permission of Mr. Diarmuid Russell; for "Road-Song of the Bandar Log" and "Seal Lullaby" from *The Jungle Book*; for the excerpt from "Sylvie and Bruno" from *Collected Verses* by Lewis Carroll; for "The Cherry Tree" from *Collected Poems* by James Stephens, by permission of the author and Macmillan & Co., Ltd.; and for "Worlds" from *Collected Poems 1905–1925* by permission of Mr. Wilfred Gibson and Macmillan & Co., Ltd.

To McClelland & Stewart, Ltd., for "Stars" and "The Fortune Seeker" by Marjorie Pickthall; for an excerpt from "The Great Lover" from *The Collected Poems of Rupert Brooke*; and for "The Wreck of the 'Julie Plante'" from *Dr. Drummond's Complete Poems* by William Henry Drummond, all by permission of McClelland & Stewart, Ltd., Publishers, Toronto, Canada.

To Methuen & Co. Ltd., for "Hay Harvest" from *Pipes and Tabors* by Patrick R. Chalmers and for "The Song of the Dog 'Quoodle'" from *The Flying Inn* by Gilbert Keith Chesterton.

To Alida Monro and the Poetry Bookshop for "Milk for the Cat" and "Overheard on a Saltmarsh" by Harold Monro.

To William Morrow & Co., for "Beauty" from *I Am a Pueblo Indian Girl* by E-Yeh-Shure, copyright, 1938, by William Morrow & Co., by permission of William Morrow & Co., Inc.

To John Murray for "A Soft Day" by Winifred M. Letts.

To Francis Newbolt for "Egypt's Might is Tumbled Down" by Mary E. Coleridge from *Poems,* published by Messrs. Elkin Mathews and Marrot (now Messrs. George Allen & Unwin).

To the Newman Book Shop for "To a Snowflake" by Francis Thompson.

To *The New Yorker.* The poem "Epitaph for a Persian Kitten" (page 46) and "The Uncharted" (page 375) originally appeared in *The New Yorker;* Copyright, 1931 and 1942, respectively, by The F-R Publishing Corporation.

To Bridget M. O'Connell for "A Tutor Who Tooted the Flute" by Carolyn Wells.

To Oliver & Boyd Ltd., for "Blessing of the Kindling" from *Carmina Gadelica* edited by J. Carmichael Watson.

To Oxford University Press for "Glory be to God for dappled things" from *Pied Beauty* by Gerard Manley Hopkins, by permission of the poet's family; for "Big Steamers" and "The Dawn Wind" by Rudyard Kipling from *A History of England* by C. R. L. Fletcher and Rudyard Kipling.

To Theodore Presser Co. for "The Wraggle Taggle Gipsies O!" from *One Hundred English Folk-Songs,* compiled and edited by Cecil Sharp.

To The Royal Irish Academy for the excerpt from *Todd Lectures Vol. 15;* "The Instructions of King Cormac MacAirt," Kuno Meyer, 1909, published by the Royal Irish Academy.

To The Ryerson Press for "A January Morning" from *Lyrics of Earth* by Archibald Lampman. By permission of The Ryerson Press, Toronto, Canada.

To Sands & Co., Ltd., for "Highland Fairies" by J. B. Salmond.

To Siegfried Sassoon for his poem "Everyone Sang."

To *The Saturday Review of Literature* for "Connecticut Rondel" by Marion Canby.

To E. C. Schirmer Music Co. for "The Coasts of High Barbary" from *The Home and Community Song Book.*

To G. Schirmer, Inc. for "I Wash My Face in a Golden Vase," "Never Was a Child so Lovely," "Riddles Wisely Expounded," "The Farmer's Curst Wife," "The Milk-Maid," and "The Weep-Willow Tree" from *Ballads, Carols, and Tragic Legends from the Southern Appalachian Mountains* by John Jacob Niles. Copyright, 1937, by G.

Acknowledgments

Schirmer, Inc.; for "John Henry" and "There Was an Old Woman" from *More Songs of the Hill-Folk* by John Jacob Niles. Copyright, 1936, by G. Schirmer, Inc.; for "Kentucky Wassail Song" and "The Three Little Pigs" from *Songs of the Hill-Folk* by John Jacob Niles. Copyright, 1934, by G. Schirmer Inc.

To Charles Scribner's Sons for "Bright is the Ring of Words," "Envoy," "I Will Make You Brooches," and "Winter" by Robert Louis Stevenson from *Songs of Travel and Other Poems*; for "Carol" and "Ducks' Ditty": Reprinted from *The Wind in the Willows* by Kenneth Grahame; copyright, 1908, 1935, by Charles Scribner's Sons; used by permission of the publisher; and for "The Rainy Summer" from *Early Poems* by Alice Meynell.

To Martin Secker & Warburg for "Mrs. Reece Laughs" by Martin Armstrong and for "The Old Ships" by James Elroy Flecker.

To Selwyn & Blount, Ltd., for "Last Song" from *The Wild Garden* by James Guthrie and for "November Skies" by John Freeman.

To Noel F. Sharp for "An Almanac" and "The Field Mouse" from *Poems* by William Sharp.

To Sidgwick & Jackson for "Christmas" from *A Muse at Sea* by Hilton Young, by permission of the author; and for an extract from "The Great Lover" from *Complete Poems* by Rupert Brooke, by permission of the author's representative.

To the Society of Authors and Dr. John Masefield, O.M. for permission to reprint "Cargoes"; to the Society of Authors as the Literary Representative of the Estate of the late A. E. Housman, and Messrs. Jonathan Cape, Ltd., publishers of A. E. Housman's *Collected Works* for "Loveliest of Trees," "Reveille," "The Night is Freezing Fast," and "Yonder See the Morning Blink"; and to the Society of Authors and Mrs. Binyon for "The Little Dancers: A London Vision" from *Collected Poems* by Laurence Binyon.

To J. C. Squire, for his poem "Sonnet" taken from *Poems: First Series*.

To James Stephens for his poems, "April Showers," "Breakfast Time," "Little Things," "Seamus Beg," "The Fifteen Acres," "The Rivals," "The Voice of God," "Washed in Silver," and "White Fields."

To Helen Thomas and Faber & Faber Ltd., for "Digging" by Edward Thomas.

To The Viking Press, Inc., for "All Mothers Speak to Mary" from *The Long Christmas* by Ruth Sawyer. Copyright, 1941, by Ruth Sawyer. By permission of The Viking Press, Inc., New York; for "Eeka, Neeka," "The Old Tailor," "The Prince," "The Snowflake," and "Where" from *Bells and Grass* by Walter de la Mare. Copyright, 1942, by Walter de la Mare; for "Nosegay for a Young Goat" from *Blossoming Antlers* by Winifred Welles. Copyright, 1933, by Winifred Welles; for "Number Song" from *Under the Tree* by Elizabeth Madox Roberts. Copyright, 1922, by B. W. Huebsch, Inc.; for "The Creation" from *God's Trombones* by James Weldon Johnson. Copyright, 1927, by The Viking Press, Inc.

To Frederick Warne & Co., Ltd.. for "Calico Pie" from *Nonsense Songs* by Edward Lear and for "There Was an Old Man with a Beard" from *The Book of Nonsense* by Edward Lear.

To A. P. Watt & Son for "Big Steamers" and "The Dawn Wind" by Rudyard Kipling from *A History of England* by C. R. L. Fletcher and Rudyard Kipling, by permission of Mrs. George Bambridge; to A. P. Watt and Mrs. W. B. Yeats for "Aedh Wishes for the Cloths of Heaven," "The Lake Isle of Innisfree," and "The Song of the Wandering Aengus" from *Collected Poems of W. B. Yeats*; for "In February" from *George MacDonald's Poetical Works*, with permission of the executors of George MacDonald; to A. P. Watt and Mrs. George Bambridge for "Road-Song of the Bandar Log" and "Seal Lullaby" from *The Jungle Book*, published by Macmillan & Co., Ltd.,

Acknowledgments

for "A Song of Sherwood" from *The Collected Poems of Alfred Noyes*, by permission of Alfred Noyes; to A. P. Watt and the executrix of the late Mr. G. K. Chesterton for "Song of the Dog 'Quoodle'" from *The Flying Inn*; for "The Old Ships" from *The Collected Poems of James Elroy Flecker* by permission of Mrs. Flecker and Messrs. Martin Secker & Warburg, publishers.

No effort has been spared to trace copyright and ownership of all poems included in these pages. If the editors have failed in any case, however, to fulfill their intention of obtaining permission to reprint and of making full acknowledgment, they offer regretful apologies and warm thanks.

The work of authenticating the material of this collection has been made immeasurably less difficult by the generous services of a great many people. To all of them we express our lively appreciation; in particular to:

Mildred Ostvold of the Winnetka Public Library, for valuable assistance in copyright research; and to other members of the Winnetka Public Library staff for resourceful cooperation in verifying a variety of necessary details.

Ruth Wilcox, Barbara Penyak and other staff members of the Fine Arts Division of the Cleveland Public Library, for assistance in authenticating the Index of Musical Settings.

Dr. Charles R. Sanderson, Chief Librarian, and the staff of the Reference Department of the Public Library of Toronto, Canada, for help in tracing the source and correct forms of many British poems; and to Lillian Smith, Head of The Boys' and Girls' House of the Public Library of Toronto, for verifying the form and source of two poems.

Dr. Marius Barbeau, of the National Museum, Ottawa, Canada; and John Murray Gibbon, for extensive information in the matter of Canadian folk-song material, with special reference to "The Song of the Dawn."

INDEX OF AUTHORS AND SOURCES

Index of Authors and Sources

Index of Authors and Sources

400

INDEX OF FIRST LINES

Index of First Lines

404

Index of First Lines

INDEX OF MUSICAL SETTINGS

Since singing is so good a thing,
I wish all men would learn to sing.
— *William Byrd (1542–1623)*

Aedh Wishes for the Cloths of Heaven (W. B. Yeats) Thomas F. Dunhill. Curwen, London; G. Schirmer, New York

As Joseph Was A-Walking (Traditional) CHRISTMAS CAROLS edited by Walter. Macmillan, London and New York. THE CONCORD HYMNAL compiled by Huntington & Robinson. E. C. Schirmer, Boston; J. & W. Chester, London

Bells of London, The (Traditional) Traditional tune: 'Oranges and Lemons.' THE BABY'S OPERA compiled by Crane. Frederick Warne, London and New York

Calico Pie (Edward Lear) Four-part Choral Song: George Ingraham. G. Schirmer, New York; Chappell & Co., London

Ceremonies for Candlemasse Eve (Robert Herrick) Tune from An Old Church Gallery-Book. THE OXFORD BOOK OF CAROLS edited by Dearmer, Vaughan Williams & Shaw. Oxford Press, London; Carl Fischer, New York

Christmas (E. Hilton Young) Unison Choral Song: Lilian Smith. Oxford Press, London; Carl Fischer, New York

Coasts of High Barbary, The (Traditional) THE HOME AND COMMUNITY SONG BOOK edited by Surette & Davison. E. C. Schirmer, Boston; J. & W. Chester, London

Dabbling in the Dew (Traditional) A BOOK OF SONGS edited by Davison, Surette & Zanzig. E. C. Schirmer, Boston; J. & W. Chester, London. ONE HUNDRED ENGLISH FOLK SONGS edited by Sharp. Oliver Ditson, Philadelphia

Derby Ram, The (Traditional) ENGLISH COUNTY SONGS edited by Broadwood & Fuller Maitland. J. B. Cramer, London; Edward Schuberth, New York

Easter (George Herbert) Sung to Choral Tune by J. S. Bach. TWENTY-FIVE CHORALS by J. S. Bach. E. C. Schirmer, Boston; J. & W. Chester, London

from *Evening Quatrains* (Charles Cotton) Two-part Choral Song by W. Gillies Whittaker. Oxford Press, London; Carl Fischer, New York

Farmer's Curst Wife, The (Traditional) Traditional tune. SONGS OF THE HILL FOLK collected by Niles. G. Schirmer, New York; Chappell & Co., London

Four Presents, The (Traditional) Traditional tune. THE BABY'S BOUQUET compiled by Crane. Frederick Warne, London and New York

God Be in My Hede (13th Century, Unknown) Four-part Hymn: R. O. Morris. SONGS OF PRAISE edited by Vaughan Williams. Oxford Press, London; Carl Fischer, New York. Traditional Choral Strophe: arranged and harmonized by Harrington Shortall. HYMNS FOR WORSHIP, Association Press, New York

Great Time, A (W. H. Davies) Michael Head. Boosey & Hawkes, London and New York

Green Broom (Traditional) Traditional tune. COLLECTED FOLK SONGS edited by Sharp & Vaughan Williams. Novello, London; H. W. Gray, New York

Green Grow the Rushes (Traditional) Traditional tune. ENGLISH COUNTY SONGS edited by Broadwood & Fuller Maitland. J. B. Cramer, London; Edward Schuberth, New York. FIRESIDE BOOK OF FOLK SONGS edited by Boni. Simon & Schuster, New York

I Know Where I'm Going (Modern Irish, Unknown) Composer unknown. IRISH

407

Index of Musical Settings

COUNTRY SONGS, Vol. I, edited by Hughes. Boosey & Hawkes, London and New York

I Love All Beauteous Things (Robert Bridges) Harold E. Darke. Oxford Press, London; Carl Fischer, New York

I Wash My Face in a Golden Vase (Traditional) Traditional tune. BALLADS, CAROLS AND TRAGIC LEGENDS FROM THE SOUTHERN APPALACHIAN MOUNTAINS collected by Niles. G. Schirmer, New York; Chappell & Co., London

Jerusalem (William Blake) Unison Choral Song: C. Hubert H. Parry. SONGS OF PRAISE edited by Vaughan Williams. Oxford Press, London; Carl Fischer, New York

John Gilpin (William Cowper) E. Duncan. THE MINSTRELSY OF ENGLAND, Vol. II. Augener, London; Broude Brothers, New York

John Henry (Traditional) Traditional tune. MORE SONGS OF THE HILL FOLK collected by Niles. G. Schirmer, New York; Chappell & Co., London

Kentucky Wassail Song, The (Traditional) Traditional tune. SONGS OF THE HILL FOLK collected by Niles. G. Schirmer, New York; Chappell & Co., London

Keys of Canterbury, The (Traditional) Traditional tune. ONE HUNDRED ENGLISH FOLK SONGS edited by Sharp. Oliver Ditson, Philadelphia

Lamb, The (William Blake) Unison Choral Song: Rutland Boughton. SIX UNISON SONGS by Rutland Boughton. Novello, London; H. W. Gray, New York

Let Us Now Praise Famous Men (Apocrypha) Unison Choral Song: R. Vaughan Williams. Curwen, London; G. Schirmer, New York

Little Disaster, The (Traditional) Traditional tune. THE BABY'S BOUQUET compiled by Crane. Frederick Warne, London and New York

Little Things (James Stephens) Melody from ANDERNACH GESANGBUCH, 1608 (adapted). SONGS OF PRAISE edited by Vaughan Williams. Oxford Press, London; Carl Fischer, New York

Matthew, Mark, Luke and John (Traditional) Traditional tune. SONGS OF THE WEST, Revised Edition, edited by Sharp. Methuen, London

Mayers' Song, The (Traditional) Traditional tune: 'The Bellman's Song.' THE OXFORD BOOK OF CAROLS edited by Dearmer, Vaughan Williams & Shaw. Oxford Press, London; Carl Fischer, New York

Merry Are the Bells (Traditional) Unison Choral Song: Maynard Grover. Oxford Press, London; Carl Fischer, New York

Milk-Maid, The (Traditional) Traditional tune. BALLADS, LOVE-SONGS AND TRAGIC LEGENDS FROM THE SOUTHERN APPALACHIAN MOUNTAINS collected by Niles. G. Schirmer, New York; Chappell & Co., London

My Heart's in the Highlands (Robert Burns) Ancient Gaelic Air, in Fraser's AIRS, as 'Crodh Chailean,' 1816. SONGS OF SCOTLAND, compiled and arranged by Lampe. J. H. Remick, New York

Nancy Hanks (Rosemary and Stephen Vincent Benét) Choral Song for Women's Voices: Katherine K. Davis. Galaxy, New York

Never Was a Child So Lovely (Traditional) Traditional tune. BALLADS, CAROLS AND TRAGIC LEGENDS FROM THE SOUTHERN APPALACHIAN MOUNTAINS collected by Niles. G. Schirmer, New York; Chappell & Co., London

O Mistress Mine (William Shakespeare) Melody from Queen Elizabeth's Virginal Book, 1611. FIFTY SHAKESPEARE SONGS edited by Vincent. Oliver Ditson, Philadelphia. PAN PIPES arranged by Marzials. Frederick Warne, London and New York

Old Woman of the Roads, An (Padraic Colum) Unison Choral Song: Percy Judd. Oxford Press, London; Carl Fischer, New York

Index of Musical Settings

On May Morning (John Milton) Two-part Choral Song: Norman F. Demuth. Oxford Press, London; Carl Fischer, New York

'Over Hill, Over Dale' (William Shakespeare) Thomas Simpson Cook. SONGS OF ENGLAND, Vol. III, edited by Hatton & Fanning. Boosey & Hawkes, London and New York

Pack, Clouds, Away (Thomas Heywood) Choral Part-song: Grace Wilbur Conant. TWENTY PART-SONGS FOR MIXED VOICES compiled by Clough-Leighter. Oliver Ditson, Philadelphia

Peace (Henry Vaughan) Melody by Melchior Vulpius, adapted and harmonized by J. S. Bach. SONGS OF PRAISE edited by Vaughan Williams. Oxford Press, London; Carl Fischer, New York

Ploughboy in Luck, The (Traditional) Traditional tune. THE BABY'S OPERA compiled by Crane. Frederick Warne, London and New York

Riddles Wisely Expounded (Traditional) Traditional tune. BALLADS, CAROLS AND TRAGIC LEGENDS FROM THE SOUTHERN APPALACHIAN MOUNTAINS collected by Niles. G. Schirmer, New York; Chappell & Co., London

Saint Patrick's Breastplate (translated by Kuno Meyer) Four-part Choral Song: Arnold Bax. Murdoch, Murdoch & Co., London; E. C. Schirmer, Boston

from *Shepherds Hymn Their Saviour* (Richard Crashaw) Choral Tune by J. S. Bach. TWENTY-FIVE CHORALS by J. S. Bach. E. C. Schirmer, Boston; J. & W. Chester, London

'Some Say . . .' (William Shakespeare) Unison Choral Song, 'The Gracious Time': Robin Milford. Oxford Press, London; Carl Fischer, New York

Song: *'Tell Me Where Is Fancy Bred'* (William Shakespeare) Thomas Arne. ONE HUNDRED SONGS OF ENGLAND edited by Bantock. Oliver Ditson, Philadelphia

Song of Master Valiant-for-Truth, The (John Bunyan) Traditional tune: 'Monk's Gate.' SONGS OF PRAISE edited by Vaughan Williams. Oxford Press, London; Carl Fischer, New York

Song of Sherwood, A (Alfred Noyes) Unison Choral Song: James H. Rogers. SONGS OF MANY LANDS AND PEOPLES edited by McConathy, Beattie & Morgan. Silver Burdett, New York

Song of the Watchmen (attributed to James Fortescue) Traditional tune: 'The London Waits.' A BOOK OF SONGS edited by Davison, Surette & Zanzig. E. C. Schirmer, Boston; J. & W. Chester, London

Souling Song, The (Traditional) Traditional tune. ENGLISH COUNTY SONGS edited by Broadwood & Fuller Maitland. J. B. Cramer, London; Edward Schuberth, New York

Spring (William Blake) Unison Choral Song: Rutland Boughton. SIX UNISON SONGS by Rutland Boughton. Novello, London; H. W. Gray, New York

There Was an Old Woman (Traditional) Traditional tune. MORE SONGS OF THE HILL FOLK collected by Niles. G. Schirmer, New York; Chappell & Co., London

Thomas Rymer (Traditional) Traditional tune. BALLADS OF BRITAIN edited by Goss. John Lane, London

Three Little Pigs, The (Traditional) Traditional tune. SONGS OF THE HILL FOLK collected by Niles. G. Schirmer, New York; Chappell & Co., London

Three Ships, The (Traditional) Choral Song for Mixed Voices, 'The Sycamore Tree': Peter Warlock. Oxford Press, London; Carl Fischer, New York

from THROUGH THE LOOKING-GLASS (Lewis Carroll) Sung to 'My Harp and My Lute': Henry Bishop. THE MINSTRELSY OF ENGLAND, Vol. I. Augener, London; Broude Bros., New York

Index of Musical Settings

Weathers (Thomas Hardy) Unison Choral Song: Robin Milford. Oxford Press, London; Carl Fischer, New York

Weep-Willow Tree, The (Traditional) Traditional tune. BALLADS, LOVE-SONGS AND TRAGIC LEGENDS FROM THE SOUTHERN APPALACHIAN MOUNTAINS collected by Niles. G. Schirmer, New York; Chappell & Co., London

Whale, The (Traditional) Traditional tune. SEA SONGS edited by Whall. Brown & Son, Ferguson, Glasgow

Widdicombe Fair (Traditional) Traditional tune. A BOOK OF SONGS edited by Davison, Surette & Zanzig. E. C. Schirmer, Boston; J. & W. Chester, London. FIRESIDE BOOK OF FOLK SONGS edited by Boni. Simon & Schuster, New York

Wraggle Taggle Gipsies O!, The (Traditional) Traditional tune. ONE HUNDRED ENGLISH FOLK SONGS edited by Sharp. Oliver Ditson, Philadelphia. FIRESIDE BOOK OF FOLK SONGS edited by Boni. Simon & Schuster, New York

INDEX OF TITLES

411

Index of Titles

412

Index of Titles

414